Kids' Birthday
Cakes
Step by Step

Kids' Birthday Cakes Step by Step

Karen Sullivan

LONDON, NEW YORK, MELBOURNE,
MUNICH, AND DELHI

Project Editor Kathy Woolley
Designer Harriet Yeomans
Managing Editor Dawn Henderson
Managing Art Editor Christine Keilty
Jacket Art Editor Kathryn Wilding
Senior Producer, Pre-Production Tony Phipps
Senior Producer Jen Scothern
Art Director Peter Luff
Publisher Peggy Vance

Cake Decorators Sandra Monger, Hannah
Wiltshire, Kasey Clarke, Juniper Cakery

DK INDIA
Project Editor Bushra Ahmed
Senior Art Editor Ira Sharma
Editor Ligi John
Art Editor Simran Kaur
Assistant Art Editor Sourabh Challariya
Managing Editor Alicia Ingty
Managing Art Editor Navidita Thapa
Pre-Production Manager Sunil Sharma
DTP Designers Rajdeep Singh,
Manish Upreti, Mohammad Usman

First published in Great Britain in 2014 by
Dorling Kindersley Limited
80 Strand, London, WC2R ORL
Penguin Group (UK)

Copyright © 2014 Dorling Kindersley
2 4 6 8 10 9 7 5 3 1
001 – 259429 – Aug/2014

A CIP catalogue record for this book is available
from the British Library

ISBN: 978-1-4093-5719-3

Colour reproduction by Altaimage LTD
Printed and bound in South China

Discover more at **www.dk.com**

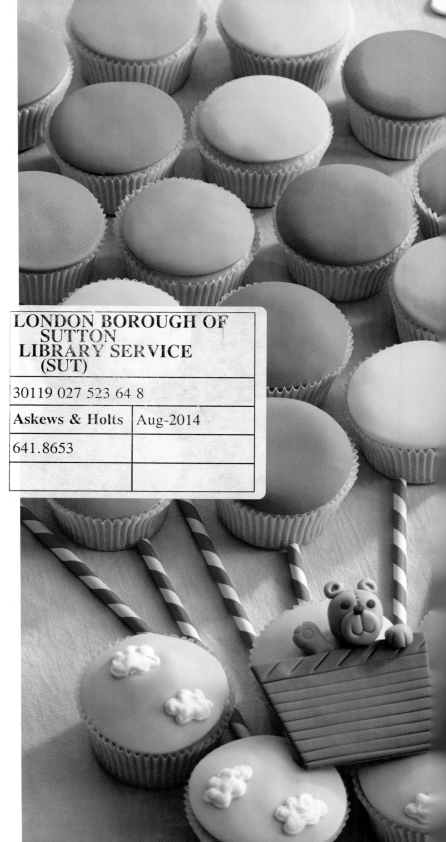

Contents

Introduction

It's never been easier to bake and decorate delicious, imaginative, and truly child-friendly cakes, and with all the ingredients and tools you need now readily available, even amateur decorators can create show-stopping cakes, cupcakes, and cake pops with ease. There is something hugely satisfying about producing homemade creations, designed to match a party theme and your child's individual interests, and this book offers not just detailed, step-by-step instructions to achieve something truly spectacular, but inspiration for producing your own designs and variations, too.

Everything from **basic baking techniques**, levelling, icing, and filling cakes to delicious recipes, covering a cake drum, dipping and decorating cake pops and producing perfect cupcakes is given the step-by-step treatment. Twenty amazing **cake projects**, complete with variations and suggestions for party favours or additional treats to enhance your theme, top the bill, and you'll discover how to create an astonishing range of children's birthday cakes from scratch.

Everyone from **absolute beginners** to **seasoned experts** will find cakes to suit their level of skill and experience, and inspiration to produce their own creations. If you want to make something easy but stunning you'll love the gorgeous Sparkly Butterfly, Fish Tank Friends, Up, Up, and Away, Cupcake Owl, Cupcake Caterpillar, Over the Rainbow, Football Mania, Treasure Island, Over the Moon, and Monster Madness cakes. Bakers with a little more time on their hands will find the stunning In the Jungle, Pretty Fairies, Dinosaur Egg, Flying Superhero, Circus Big Top, Party Train, Princess Castle, Happy Robot, Prima Ballerina, and Furry Teddy Bear cakes a satisfying challenge. You'll find cakes for footie fans, monster-mad tots, budding superheroes, train buffs, space fanatics, dinosaur hunters, shipwrecked pirates, robot engineers and even fairy princesses. Choose your cake, gather your equipment and ingredients, and we'll guide you through every step until you achieve the cake of your child's dreams.

You'll find inspiring ideas for cake pops, cupcakes, and round cakes on the dedicated **feature pages**, as well as a number of 10-minute transformations that will help you produce a masterpiece with a few simple ideas (and cheats). Now is the time to learn how to bake and decorate cakes that will please a crowd and thrill the birthday boy or girl.

Enjoy!

Cake Chooser

From simple projects to... > > > > > > > > > > > > > >

Cupcake Caterpillar *p142*

Sparkly Butterfly *p126*

Cupcake Owl *p82*

Up, Up, and Away *p28*

Monster Madness *p12*

Fish Tank Friends *p112*

Over the Rainbow *p60*

Football Mania *p96*

Prima Ballerina *p104*

Over the Moon *p34*

Happy Robot *p120*

Flying Superhero p154

Dinosaur Egg p74

Treasure Island p50

Furry Teddy Bear p42

  Cake Chooser

Princess Castle *p146*

Party Train *p66*

Pretty Fairies *p20*

Circus Big Top *p130*

In the Jungle *p86*

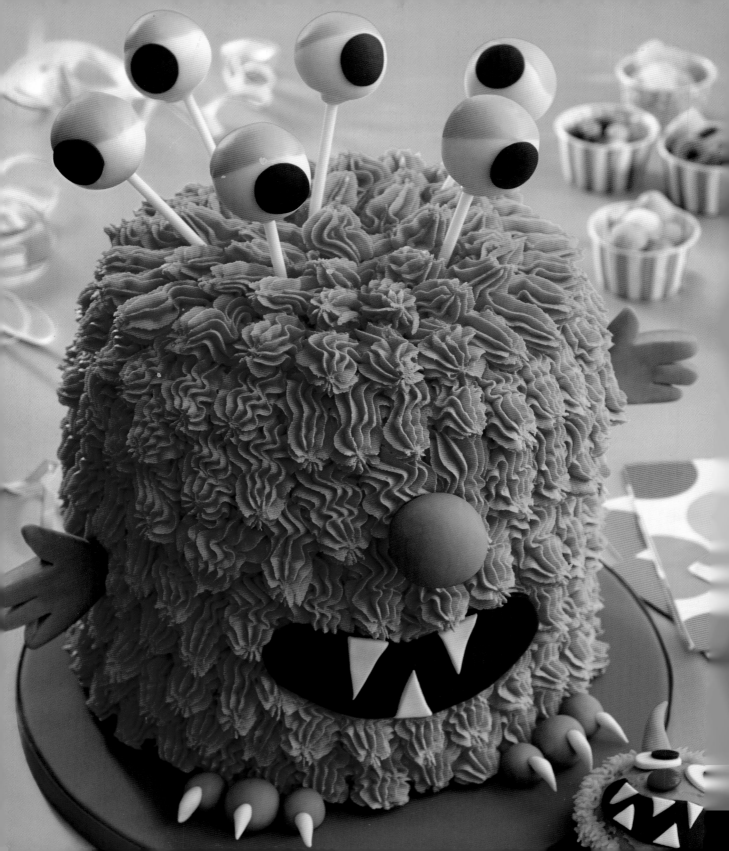

Monster Madness

Frighten your party guests with this cheeky six-eyed monster, complete with piped buttercream fur, a bright green nose, fierce teeth, and neat little toes. The cake is stacked, but does not need dowels for support. Accompany with the monster cupcakes on page 18 – if you dare.

 PREP 1½ hrs   **BAKE** 2 hrs   **DECORATE** 2¼ hrs, plus overnight drying time   **SERVES** 30

Ingredients

- 4 x 20cm (8in) round vanilla sponge cakes (see p164)
- 18cm (7in) vanilla sponge cake
- 1kg (2¼lb) vanilla buttercream icing (see p180)
- cornflour, for dusting
- 300g (10oz) bright-blue fondant, strengthened (see p176)
- orange colouring paste
- 250g (9oz) white candy melts
- 6 x 30g (1oz) cake pops (see pp172–3)
- 100g (3½oz) orange candy melts
- 50g (1¾oz) black fondant
- 50g (1¾oz) white fondant
- 100g (3½oz) green fondant, strengthened

Equipment

- 30cm (12in) cake board
- palette knife
- 30cm (12in) round cake drum
- fondant roller and smoother
- sharp knife
- large star piping nozzle (PME no. 13)
- large piping bag
- 9 cake-pop sticks
- polystyrene (optional)
- 3cm (1¼in) circular cutter
- 1m (3¼ft) green satin ribbon, 1cm (½in) wide
- craft glue

1 To construct the layers, place one of the 20cm (8in) sponges on the cake board. Using a palette knife, cover the top with a layer of buttercream icing, then place the second cake on it. Continue until you have stacked all four 20cm (8in) cakes. Apply a layer of buttercream icing to the top of the stack and position the smaller cake on it. Crumb coat the entire cake with buttercream icing (see p171) and set aside overnight.

2 To cover the cake drum, dust a surface with cornflour and roll out the bright-blue fondant in a circle large enough to cover the cake drum – it should be about 3mm (⅛in) thick. Brush the drum with water and then carefully smooth the fondant over the surface (see p179). Polish with the fondant smoother and cut off any excess using a sharp knife. Allow to dry overnight.

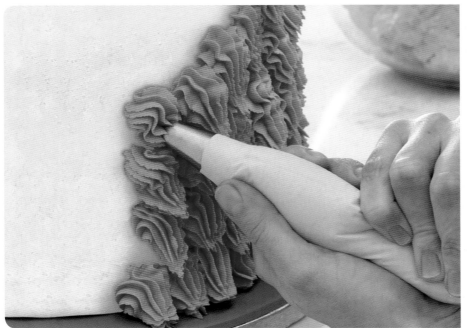

3 Move the cake to the covered drum. Colour the remaining buttercream icing using the orange colouring paste (see p180). Attach a star nozzle to the end of the piping bag and fill with the orange buttercream. Starting at the base, pipe the "fur" by pressing the bag, releasing the pressure, and pulling the icing outwards to get a nice point. Pipe moving upwards to the top edge until the cake is covered. Continue piping over the top, paying particular attention to the edges, which should appear rounded. Set aside.

4 For the eyeballs, melt the white candy melts. Insert the cake-pop sticks into the cake pops (see p173) and dip into the melted candy, coating evenly. Stand them upright in a piece of polystyrene, or an overturned colander, until they harden.

5 Melt the orange candy melts and dip each cake pop into the liquid so that they are half covered, to form the appearance of eyelids. Stand them upright again, until they are dry and hard.

Use water to
fix each circle
under the lid.

6 Dust a surface with cornflour and roll out the black fondant to about 3mm ($^1/_8$in) thick. Cut out six circles with the circular cutter and fix one on each cake pop under the lid.

7 Re-roll the remaining black fondant to about 3mm ($^1/_8$in) thick. Use a sharp knife to cut out and shape a mouth, about 10cm (4in) long and 4cm (1$^1/_2$in) wide. Set aside.

Arrange the teeth
in a random manner
to give the monster
a scary appearance.

8 Dust the surface again with cornflour and roll out a bit of the white fondant to about 3mm ($^1/_8$in) thick. Using a sharp knife, cut 3–5 triangles for the teeth. Brush the backs of the teeth with a little water and fix onto the mouth.

9 To make the toes, roll four cherry-sized balls and two slightly larger balls from the strengthened green fondant. Strengthen the remaining white fondant (see p176), and roll it into six pea-sized balls. Shape these balls into curved, pointed claws. Brush the wider ends with a little water and fix to the toes. Set aside to harden.

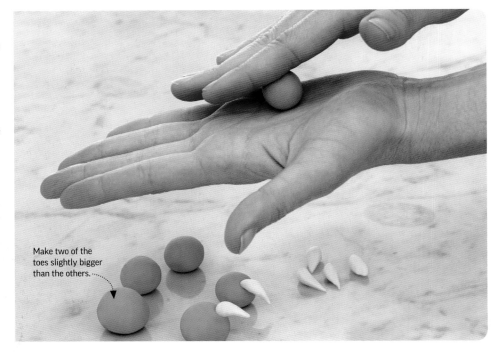

Make two of the toes slightly bigger than the others.

10 To make the nose, roll a golf-ball-sized sphere of the green fondant and insert a cake-pop stick halfway into the ball. Set aside. For the hands, roll the remaining green fondant into two walnut-sized balls and flatten slightly with the fondant roller. Cut out the fingers using a sharp knife. Moisten one end of two cake-pop sticks with a little water and insert into the wrist of each hand. Set aside to harden.

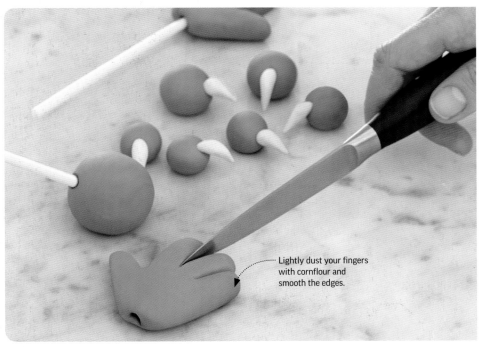

Lightly dust your fingers with cornflour and smooth the edges.

Insert the eyes at uneven angles.

Insert the hands on the sides, making sure the cake-pop sticks are not visible.

11 Moisten the back of the mouth with water and gently position on the cake. To fix the nose, moisten the stick attached to the nose and insert into the cake. Insert the cake-pop eyes into the top of the cake. Fix the green ribbon around the base of the cake drum, using a little craft glue.

Position the toes in a neat row at the base of the cake, as shown.

Monster Face Cupcakes

Using the star nozzle, pipe brightly coloured buttercream icing on to the cupcakes (see pp174–5), using the same technique as on the cake, to create furry buttercream monster faces. Use scraps of white fondant and strengthened coloured fondant to create scary teeth, eyes, noses, tentacles, and anything else that will capture your own little monsters' attention. Allow the fondant to set a little before applying to the cupcakes with water or edible glue. To provide contrast, use a palette knife to smooth the buttercream icing onto some cupcakes.

Create tentacles or horns using bright-coloured fondants.

Use the tip of a piping nozzle to score the horns.

Sandwich discs of white and black fondant onto cake pop sticks for ghoulish eye stalks.

Triangles cut from white fondant can be used to create sharp fangs

Experiment with different piping tips to create crazy fur effects with brightly coloured buttercream.

Strengthened fondant balls or candy-coated sweets can be used to create noses.

Pretty Fairies

This delicate cake is iced with soft green buttercream icing and topped with two adorable fairies, seated on fondant toadstools. Rice-paper butterflies, toadstools, and pastel blossoms are dotted around the cake and the drum, and a pretty hand-painted pattern runs around the base.

 PREP 1 hr   **BAKE** 35 mins   **DECORATE** 4-4½ hrs, plus overnight drying time   **SERVES** 20

Ingredients

- 800g (1¾lb) buttercream, tinted pale green (see p180)
- 2 x 20cm (8in) round vanilla sponge cakes (see p164), sandwiched with buttercream and crumb coated (see p171)
- dry spaghetti
- edible black pen
- cornflour, for dusting
- edible lustre dust: pink, dark green, medium green, sage green, and lilac
- rejuvenator spirit
- 4 sheets edible rice paper
- edible glitter
- 120ml (4fl oz) royal icing (see p181)
- yellow colouring paste
- 25g (scant 1oz) dark green fondant, strengthened (see p176)

For the fairies
- 100g (3½oz) flesh-coloured fondant, strengthened
- 100g (3½oz) lilac fondant, strengthened
- 100g (3½oz) yellow fondant, strengthened
- 100g (3½oz) white fondant, strengthened
- 50g (1¾oz) pale-green fondant, strengthened

continued overleaf...

1 Paddle about a quarter of the pale-green buttercream icing onto the cake drum and smooth using a palette knife. To create an even surface, dip the knife into warm water, dry, and smooth over the icing. Set the drum aside overnight for the icing to firm.

2 Set the crumb-coated cake on a sheet of greaseproof paper. Using the palette knife, apply the remaining pale-green buttercream, and then use the side scraper to achieve a smooth surface. Put to one side, ideally overnight.

- 25g (scant 1oz) brown fondant, strengthened
- 25g (scant 1oz) orange fondant, strengthened

For the toadstools
- 150g (5½oz) red fondant, strengthened
- 150g (5½oz) bright pink fondant, strengthened

Equipment

- 25cm (10in) cake drum
- palette knife
- side scraper
- sharp knife
- polystyrene
- drinking straw cut vertically in half, or smile tool
- fondant roller
- blossom plunger cutters: extra large, large, medium, and small (see p187 for templates)
- cocktail stick
- small star plunger cutter
- small fine scissors
- small artist's paintbrush
- wheel tool
- 2 piping bags
- piping nozzle (fine and medium tips, PME no. 00 and 2)
- ball tool
- small daisy plunger cutter
- 1m (3¼ft) green satin ribbon, 1cm (½in) wide
- craft glue

3 For the fairies, roll two long, thin sausages of the flesh-coloured fondant and fold each into a U-shape to create two sets of legs. Cut the ends flat, and then place on a piece of polystyrene, carefully arranging the legs so that they are crossed.

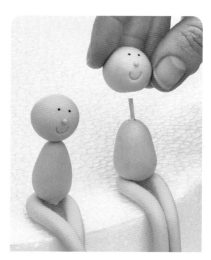

5 Fix the body of each fairy on one set of legs. Poke a hole in the base of each of the heads by placing them on the spaghetti tips protruding from the top of the body. Remove the heads and set aside to dry overnight.

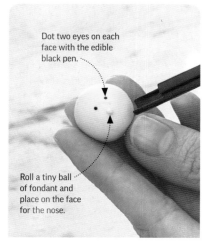

Dot two eyes on each face with the edible black pen.

Roll a tiny ball of fondant and place on the face for the nose.

4 Roll two cherry-sized balls of the flesh-coloured fondant for the heads. Score a smile using the drinking straw. For the bodies, model two bigger oval-shaped balls of the fondant. Insert a short length of spaghetti into each, leaving a bit protruding from the neck.

6 For the dresses, dust a surface with cornflour and roll out some of the lilac and yellow fondant to 2mm (¹⁄₁₆in) thick. Using the extra-large blossom cutter, cut out the skirts and score their edges using the cocktail stick.

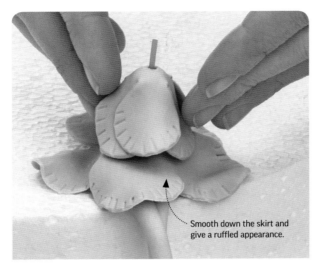

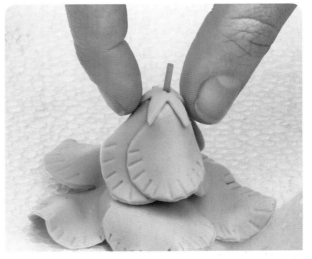

7 Cut a hole in the centre of the lilac skirt and slip it over the body. Dress the second fairy with the yellow skirt. Cut out the bodice from the lilac fondant using the large blossom cutter, and score the edges with a cocktail stick. Slip this over the body of the lilac fairy. Make a bodice for the yellow fairy using white fondant in the same way.

8 Dust a surface with cornflour and roll out the pale green fondant very thinly. Using the star plunger cutter, cut out two star collars and slip one over the top of the bodice of each fairy.

Smooth down the skirt and give a ruffled appearance.

Press an indentation into each shoe with the end of a paintbrush.

9 Roll two more long, narrow sausages of flesh-coloured fondant and cut each in half for the arms. Carefully flatten one end of each of the arms to create hands, and snip a thumb in each hand using the scissors.

10 Slip the head onto the protruding end of spaghetti. Moisten the tops of the arms with a little water and fix to the body, curving the arms and hands into position.

11 Roll two pea-sized balls of the lilac fondant and form into tiny pointed shoes. Moisten the bottom of the legs with a little water and fit into the shoes. Create yellow fondant shoes for the yellow fairy.

Pretty Fairies

Brush the cheeks with a little pink dust mixed with rejuvenator spirit.

12 For the hair, model narrow, tapered ropes of brown fondant and fix to the lilac fairy's head with a little water, with the wider ends at the crown, making a side parting. Use the wheel tool to score the surface and create individual strands, and twist and curl the hair at the base.

13 For the yellow fairy, cut two small circles of orange fondant and fix to the head with a little water. Score the surface with the wheel tool. Model a ponytail, score the surface, and fix to the back of the head at the base of the hair with a little water, and position so that it falls over one shoulder.

14 For the wings, cut out two butterfly shapes from the rice paper and dust around the edges with edible glitter. Fold in half and then open each set of wings. Pipe a line of royal icing at the fold and fix to the back of the fairies.

15 Cut out 6–7 smaller butterfly shapes from the remaining rice paper. Dust with edible glitter, fold in half, then open the wings so that they are gently curved upwards.

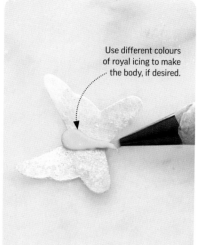

Use different colours of royal icing to make the body, if desired.

16 Tint a little of the royal icing yellow (see p181). Fit a piping bag with the no. 2 nozzle, fill with the yellow icing, and pipe the icing on the butterflies for the body. Allow to harden.

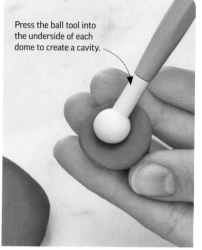

Press the ball tool into the underside of each dome to create a cavity.

17 For the toadstools, use some of the red fondant to create 6–7 cherry-sized domes to dot around the cake. Repeat using some of the bright pink fondant to make 6–7 more domes.

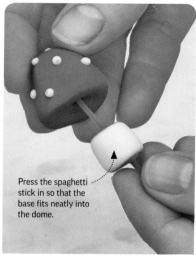

Press the spaghetti stick in so that the base fits neatly into the dome.

18 Pipe tiny dots of royal icing on the domes, and dry for 30 minutes. Form the bases using white fondant, press a piece of spaghetti into them, and fix the domes on top.

19 Use the remaining red fondant to create a larger dome for the lilac fairy to sit on. Pipe tiny dots on it using royal icing. Allow to dry and insert a piece of spaghetti into it, so it protrudes from both ends. Make a large dome using the bright pink fondant for the yellow fairy, dot with royal icing, and insert the spaghetti. Set aside to dry, ideally overnight.

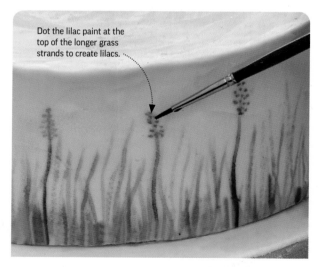

Dot the lilac paint at the top of the longer grass strands to create lilacs.

20 Carefully centre the cake on the drum. Mix together the dark green lustre dust with rejuvenator spirit and stipple foliage around the base of the cake. Repeat with the medium- and sage-green lustre dusts, until the base is covered. Mix the lilac lustre dust with rejuvenator spirit and create sprigs of tiny flowers on the cake using the paintbrush.

21 To create flowers, dust a surface with cornflour and roll out the remaining pink fondant very thinly. Using the medium and small blossom plunger cutters, cut out several little flowers. Gently curve the petals with the ball tool and pipe a dot of royal icing in the centre. Repeat with the yellow and lilac fondant until you have cut about 50 flowers.

22 On the same surface, roll out the remaining white fondant very thinly. Using the daisy plunger cutter, cut out about 60 daisies. Gently curve the petals with the ball tool and pipe a dot of the yellow royal icing in the centres.

23 Using the dark green fondant, roll about 60 teardrop-shaped leaves. Point their tips using your fingers, and score with a knife to create veins.

24 To assemble the cake, press the large toadstools into the top so that the bottom length of spaghetti goes into the cake. Dot a little royal icing on the top of the toadstools, around the spaghetti protruding from the surface, and sit the fairies on top.

25 Dot the base of the other toadstools with water and arrange on the cake and the cake drum. Fix the flowers and leaves in pretty patterns on the cake and the cake drum using a little water.

26 Use royal icing to fix the butterflies on the cake in a random pattern. Fix a yellow flower on the hair of the yellow fairy and a lilac flower on the lilac fairy with water.

27 Wrap the green satin ribbon around the cake drum and fix in place using the craft glue.

Fairytale Cupcakes

Create beautiful fairy cupcakes (see pp174–175) to accompany your magical display. Simply pipe yellow buttercream onto the surface of the cupcakes, using a large, open-star nozzle, and set to one side. Model a series of miniature toadstools, as shown in steps 17–18, and allow to dry before pressing into the buttercream. Cut out tiny blossoms in a variety of pastel colours using the small blossom plunger cutters, and pipe white royal icing in the centre.

Cut out rice paper butterflies, sprinkle with edible glitter, and fit with piped royal icing bodies before carefully displaying on the buttercream icing. Any combination of cake decorations will produce exquisite cupcakes, so use your imagination and a liberal dusting of "fairy dust" glitter.

Press the fondant toadstools onto the buttercream to decorate.

Up, Up, and Away

Multi-coloured fondant-covered cupcakes form a gorgeous balloon cake, with a modelled teddy in a basket below. An easy cake, with high impact, it uses straws to link the balloon cupcakes to the blue-sky cupcakes. You can include as many, or as few, cupcakes as you wish.

 PREP 1 hr   **BAKE** 15 mins   **DECORATE** 1–1½ hrs, plus overnight drying time   **SERVES** 24

Ingredients

- icing sugar, for dusting
- 100g (3½oz) medium-brown fondant, strengthened (see p176)
- 100g (3½oz) light-brown fondant, strengthened
- 25g (scant 1oz) dark-brown fondant
- 100g (3½oz) each yellow, orange, green, purple, and bright-blue fondant
- 75g (2½oz) red fondant
- 75g (2½oz) fuchsia fondant
- 150g (5½oz) pale-blue fondant
- 200g (7oz) buttercream icing (see p180)
- 24 vanilla sponge cupcakes (see pp164)
- 50g (1¾oz) royal icing (see p181)

Equipment

- fondant roller and smoother
- sharp knife
- blade tool
- small artist's paintbrush
- small circle-tipped piping nozzle (PME no. 2)
- Dresden tool
- cocktail stick
- 7.5cm (3in) circular cutter
- palette knife
- piping bag
- 6 straws

1 To make the basket, dust a surface with icing sugar and roll out the medium-brown fondant to 3mm (⅛in) thick. Using the sharp knife, cut a basket shape – 12cm (5in) at the top, 10cm (4in) at the bottom, and 9cm (3½in) high. Wrap the remaining fondant in cling film for later use.

2 Using the blade tool, score horizontal lines across the surface, leaving about 1cm (½in) unscored at the top of the basket. Score a series of diagonal slashes on the top of the basket and set aside to harden.

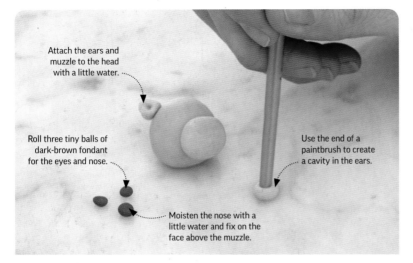

Attach the ears and muzzle to the head with a little water.

Roll three tiny balls of dark-brown fondant for the eyes and nose.

Moisten the nose with a little water and fix on the face above the muzzle.

Use the end of a paintbrush to create a cavity in the ears.

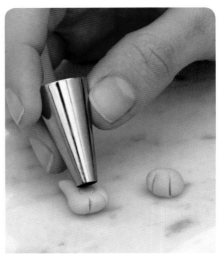

3 For the teddy, mould a walnut-sized ball of light-brown fondant for the head, and two tiny balls for the ears. Flatten the ears with your fingers, and create a cavity. Roll out a ball for the muzzle and flatten slightly. Attach the ears and muzzle to the head. Create eye sockets using the end of a paintbrush. Make the eyes and nose out of the dark-brown fondant, and place on the face. Set aside while you make the hands.

4 Form a small sausage of the light-brown fondant for the waving arm, shaping a round paw. Shape a second paw to peep over the basket. Using the blade tool, score lines on the paws, and use the piping nozzle to score a circle on the waving paw.

Use the Dresden tool to score a smile on the muzzle.

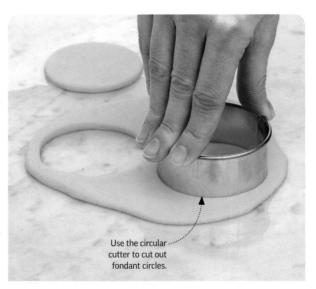

Use the circular cutter to cut out fondant circles.

5 Use the cocktail stick to create stitchmarks that run from the nose to the back of the head, between the ears. Fix the head and paws of the teddy on the basket using a little water, as shown on page 28. Set aside to dry overnight.

6 Dust a surface with icing sugar, roll out the yellow fondant to 4mm ($\frac{1}{8}$in) thick, and cut three circles. Repeat to cut three orange, three green, three purple, three bright-blue, two red, two fuchsia, and five pale-blue circles.

7 Use the palette knife to smooth a thin layer of buttercream icing on the cupcakes, about 2mm ($^1/_{16}$in) thick and not quite covering the surface. Moisten the backs of the fondant circles with a little water and press onto the surface of the iced cupcakes. Use the fondant smoother to create a smooth top.

Mini Balloon Cupcakes

Create miniature balloons to sit on top of cloud cupcakes for an extra treat. Simply dip cake pops into white candy melts (see p173), or melted white chocolate, and then quickly roll in a bowl of hundreds and thousands. Press three or four cocktail sticks (taking care to snip off the sharp ends) into each of the candy-covered pops, and allow to set.

Once hard, invert and press into the cloud cupcakes (see step 8). You can also create balloons from cake pops dipped in a variety of brightly coloured candy melts, to liven up your display. Or make some tiny fondant teddies or baskets to sit under the balloon.

8 To make the sky, use the small piping nozzle to pipe small dots of royal icing close together, on the blue cupcakes, to form cloud shapes. Pipe a border around them using the same tip. Allow to set before serving. Arrange the cupcakes, on a board or a presentation plate, as shown on page 28.

10-minute *transformations*

You can transform a basic cake in just minutes with these simple but effective ideas. Start with a sponge cake iced with buttercream then create the perfect party centrepiece with a selection of shop-bought sweets and toys, a little imagination, and a lot of style.

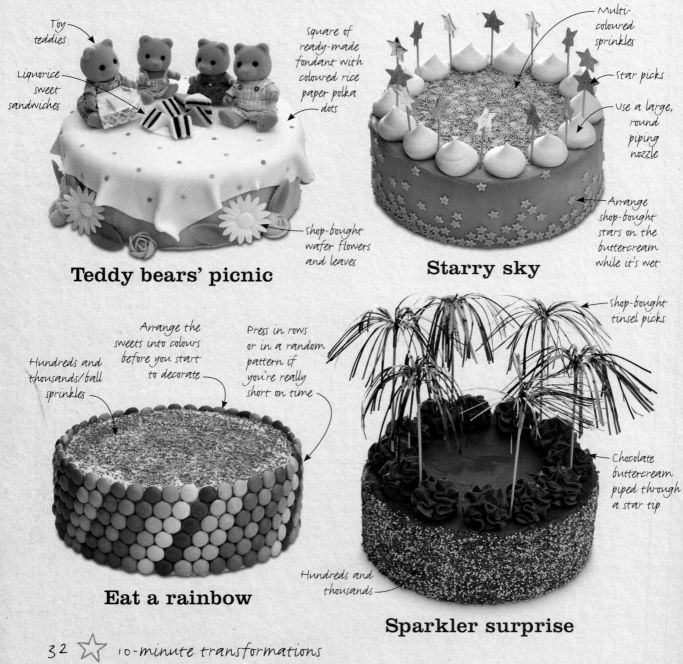

Toy teddies

Liquorice sweet sandwiches

square of ready-made fondant with coloured rice paper polka dots

shop-bought wafer flowers and leaves

Teddy bears' picnic

Multi-coloured sprinkles

star picks

Use a large, round piping nozzle

Arrange shop-bought stars on the buttercream while it's wet

Starry sky

Arrange the sweets into colours before you start to decorate

Press in rows or in a random pattern if you're really short on time

Hundreds and thousands/ball sprinkles

Eat a rainbow

shop-bought tinsel picks

Chocolate buttercream piped through a star tip

Hundreds and thousands

Sparkler surprise

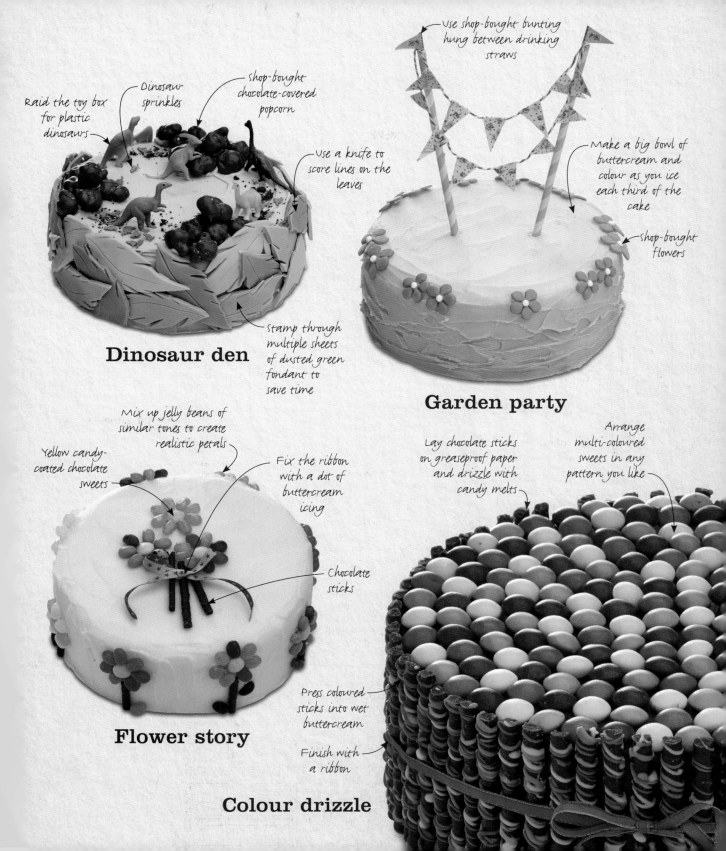

Dinosaur den

Raid the toy box for plastic dinosaurs

Dinosaur sprinkles

shop-bought chocolate-covered popcorn

Use a knife to score lines on the leaves

Stamp through multiple sheets of dusted green fondant to save time

Garden party

Use shop-bought bunting hung between drinking straws

Make a big bowl of buttercream and colour as you ice each third of the cake

shop-bought flowers

Flower story

Mix up jelly beans of similar tones to create realistic petals

Yellow candy-coated chocolate sweets

Fix the ribbon with a dot of buttercream icing

Chocolate sticks

Colour drizzle

Lay chocolate sticks on greaseproof paper and drizzle with candy melts

Arrange multi-coloured sweets in any pattern you like

Press coloured sticks into wet buttercream

Finish with a ribbon

Over the Moon

Blast off with this brilliant space cake, accessorized with planetary cake pops, eerie green aliens, and glittery gold stars. The fondant rocket is easy to make and will last for months in an airtight container, so your little space travellers can admire it long after the festivities have ended.

PREP 1 hr   **BAKE** 45 mins   **DECORATE** 3¾ hrs, plus overnight drying time   **SERVES** 20

Ingredients

- cornflour, for dusting
- 500g (1lb 2oz) black fondant 200g (7oz) yellow fondant
- gold lustre dust mixed with rejuvenator spirit, or gold lustre spray (optional)
- silver dragées
- 1kg (2¼lb) vanilla buttercream, half tinted dark grey, half tinted light grey (see p180)
- 20cm (8in) dome cake (see p187) (made in half of a hemisphere or ball tin), crumb coated with buttercream (see p171)

For the aliens
- 500g (1lb 2oz) alien green fondant, strengthened (see p176)
- dry spaghetti
- 25g (scant 1oz) white fondant
- 25g (scant 1oz) black fondant

For the rocket
- 30g (1oz) red fondant, strengthened
- 100g (3½oz) blue fondant, strengthened
- 25g (scant 1oz) grey fondant, strengthened
- 25g (scant 1oz) yellow fondant, strengthened
- silver lustre spray

continued overleaf...

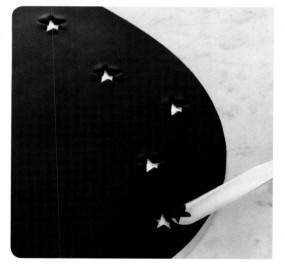

1 Using a fondant roller, roll the black fondant to about 3mm (⅛in) thick in a circle large enough to cover the drum. Brush the drum lightly with water and cover with the fondant (see p179). Cut off any excess with a sharp knife and reserve the remaining fondant. Carefully cut out about 15 stars from the around the edge of the circle, using the star cutter. Lift them from the drum using a palette knife and discard.

2 To make the aliens, mould a cherry-sized ball of the strengthened alien green fondant into a cone and then model into a gentle teardrop shape. Repeat to make three aliens. To create the larger alien, use a golf-ball-sized ball of green fondant and mould into a teardrop shape. Using scissors, snip three peaks on the top and use your fingers to smooth.

- 25g (scant 1oz) royal icing (see p181)
- 25g (scant 1oz) orange fondant

Equipment

- fondant roller and smoother
- 30cm (12in) cake drum
- sharp knife
- 1.2cm (³⁄₈in) star cutter
- palette knife
- 4 circular cutters – 1.2cm (³⁄₄in), 4cm (1½in), 2.5cm (1in), and 5mm (¼in)
- piping nozzle (PME no. 2)
- small artist's paintbrush
- cake-pop stick
- 10 x 24-gauge silver wires
- 1m (3¼ft) black satin ribbon, 1cm (½in) wide
- craft glue
- plastic flower pick

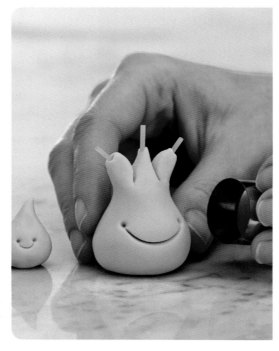

3 Insert small pieces of dry spaghetti into the peaks to create spikes. These will support the eyeballs. Use a circular cutter to emboss smiles on the aliens. The end of a paintbrush can be used to mark the corners of the aliens' mouths.

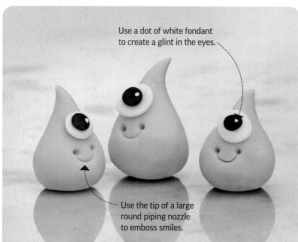

Use a dot of white fondant to create a glint in the eyes.

Use the tip of a large round piping nozzle to emboss smiles.

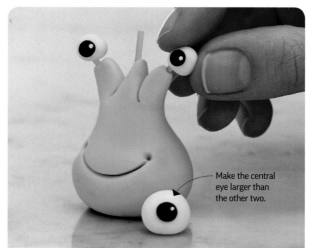

Make the central eye larger than the other two.

4 Roll three small balls of white fondant, flatten slightly, and fix on the aliens, using a little water, to create eyes. Press a smaller flattened ball of black fondant onto the surface of each ball of white fondant. Add a tiny dot of white fondant over the black fondant to create a glint in their eyes. Set aside to dry overnight.

5 For the larger alien, roll three balls of strengthened white fondant to create eyeballs, and use the same technique as in step 4 to complete the eyes. Allow to dry overnight, or until slightly hardened. When the eyeballs are firm, press them down on the alien spikes, holding them in place until they feel secure. Allow to set.

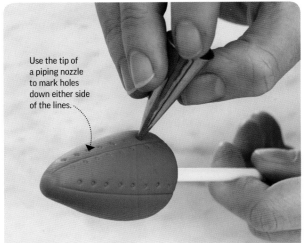

Use the tip of a piping nozzle to mark holes down either side of the lines.

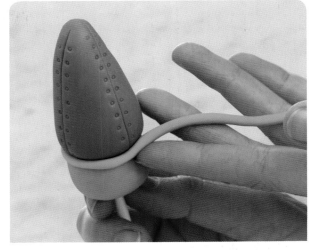

6 Begin creating the rocket by moulding an egg-shaped ball of strengthened red fondant into an elongated cone shape. Moisten the end of a cake-pop stick and press into the base. This will support the rocket above the cake. While the fondant is still slightly soft, use the back of a knife to emboss three lines from the point of the rocket down to the base.

7 Mould a base to fit the bottom of the rocket from a small ball of strengthened blue fondant. Moisten the surface with a little water and slip it onto the cake-pop stick so that it sits firmly against the red body. Roll out a thin rope of blue fondant and fix around the top of the blue base with a little water, smoothing the seam with your finger.

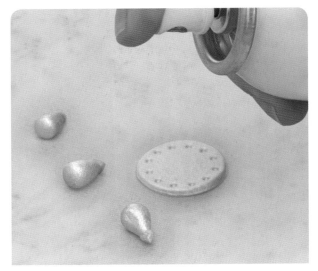

8 Roll out a little strengthened grey fondant to 2mm ($^1/_{16}$in) thick and use the 1.2cm ($^3/_4$in) circular cutter to create a porthole for the rocket. Use the piping nozzle to emboss the surface with tiny circles around the perimeter. Set aside to dry, ideally overnight.

9 Mould three pea-sized balls of grey fondant to form the exhausts. Set aside to dry, ideally overnight. Once dry, spray them with silver lustre until evenly covered – place the porthole and exhausts on a sheet of newspaper or greaseproof paper while spraying to keep the work surface clean.

10 Fix the silver exhausts to the bottom of the rocket with a little royal icing. Roll a small amount of strengthened red fondant to 2mm (1/16in) thick and cut four curved fins, using a sharp knife. Allow to dry overnight. Once hard, fix to the base of the rocket using a little royal icing.

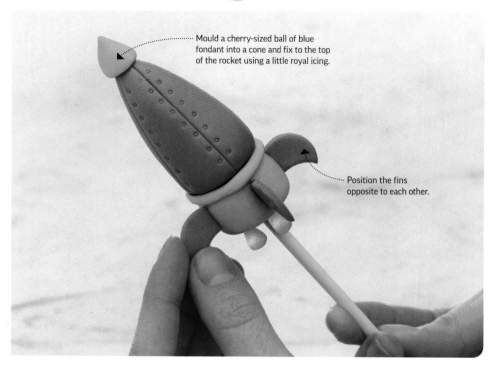

Mould a cherry-sized ball of blue fondant into a cone and fix to the top of the rocket using a little royal icing.

Position the fins opposite to each other.

11 Dust a surface with cornflour. Roll out red, yellow, and orange fondant to 2mm (1/16in) thick and cut out flame shapes using a sharp knife. Allow to dry for 1–2 days, until firm. Moisten the back of the silver porthole, and press onto the front of the rocket. Fix the flames beneath the exhausts with a little royal icing, once they are dry and completely hard.

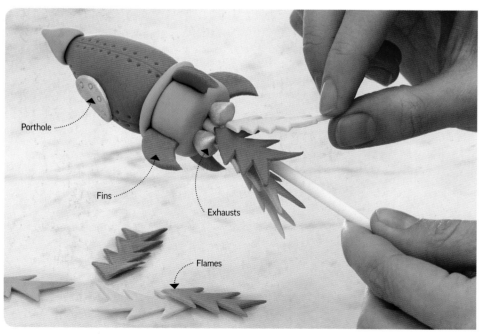

Porthole

Fins

Exhausts

Flames

 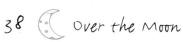

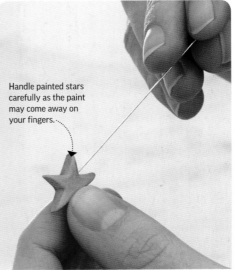

Handle painted stars carefully as the paint may come away on your fingers.

12 Dust a surface with cornflour. Roll out the yellow fondant to about 2mm ($^1/_{16}$in) thick. Use the star cutter to create 25 stars. Paint all 25 stars with the gold dust mix, or place them on a sheet of newspaper or greaseproof paper and spray with gold lustre spray. When dry, turn over and paint the other side. Allow the stars to dry for at least 1 hour.

13 Gently insert one silver wire each into 10 of the golden stars, moistening the end of the wire to secure. Set aside to dry overnight.

Silver dragées add shimmer to the covered cake drum.

14 Place the unwired stars in the pre-cut star shapes on the cake drum. Use a dot of royal icing, or apply a little water with a fine paintbrush to the silver dragées, and dot them randomly around the covered cake drum, pressing gently into the fondant surface. Secure the black ribbon around the drum with a little craft glue, and set aside to harden.

15 Place the dome cake on the drum. Using a palette knife, paddle the buttercream onto the cake to create an "ombre" effect, with one half of the dome light grey and the other half dark grey. Blend in the middle to create a blurred line where the 2 shades merge. Aim for a rippled, uneven surface.

16 Dust a surface with cornflour. Roll out the remaining black fondant to 2mm (¹/₁₆in) thick, and use the circular cutters to cut out 10–12 circles of varying sizes. Press these into the surface of the buttercream, in a random pattern, to form craters. Allow to dry.

17 Move the aliens onto the craters on the surface of the cake, moistening their bases with a little water or royal icing to glue in place. Twist the wires of the wired stars together to create an uneven spray. Poke the ends of the wired stars into a flower pick, and insert into the cake, so none of the pick is showing.

18 Insert the finished rocket into the cake, allowing it to hover over the surface on the cake-pop stick, as if blasting off.

Make sure the eyes are looking in the same direction.

Flames

You can replace strengthened fondant with flower paste – it dries harder and can be rolled out very thinly. Roll out on white vegetable fat instead of cornflour.

Roll out a rope of white fondant, flatten slightly, and fix with water.

Planet Cake Pops

Create planet cake pops for party favours or to accessorize your cake. Insert sticks into nine cake pops (see p172) and allow to set. Dip each cake pop in one colour of melted candy melt, allow to harden, and then dip and twirl in a second colour, to create a marbled effect.

Use these colour combinations: orange and white for Mercury, green and yellow for Venus, blue and green for Earth, red and orange for Mars, red and white for Jupiter, pearl white for Saturn, pale blue for Uranus, purple and blue for Neptune, and white and blue for dwarf planet Pluto.

Furry Teddy Bear

This delightful cake is the perfect centrepiece for any child's party, and is easily made using a ball cake stacked on top of carved sponge cakes. Support your furry friend with dowels and create a soft pink fondant bow to complete this cheerful teddy.

PREP 1 hr   **BAKE** 40 mins   **DECORATE** 2–3 hrs, plus overnight drying time   **SERVES** 40

Ingredients

- cornflour, for dusting
- 750g (1lb 10oz) pink fondant (see p176)
- 500g (1lb 2oz) cream fondant
- 2 x 10cm (4in) hemisphere sponge cakes (see p 186) sandwiched with vanilla buttercream and crumb coated to create a ball (see p171)
- 2 x 15cm (6in) round sponge cakes stacked and sandwiched with buttercream
- 1 x 12.5cm (5in) hemisphere cake
- 500g (1lb 2oz) vanilla buttercream (see p180)
- icing sugar, for dusting
- 1.5kg (3lb 3oz) light-brown fondant
- 25g (scant 1oz) royal icing
- 25g (scant 1oz) black fondant
- 25g (scant 1oz) brown fondant

Equipment

- fondant roller and smoother
- 30cm (12in) cake drum
- 4cm (1½in) circular cutter
- palette knife and serrated knife
- 15cm (6in) and 5cm (2in) cake boards
- wheel and ball tools
- 4 plastic dowels
- ribbon cutter, straight sides
- 1m (3¼ft) pink satin ribbon, 1cm (½in) wide
- craft glue

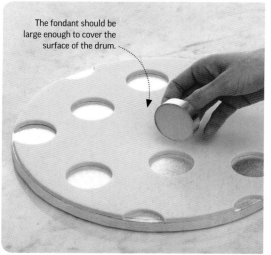

The fondant should be large enough to cover the surface of the drum.

1 Dust a surface with cornflour and roll out some of the pink fondant to 4mm (⅛in) thick. Brush the cake drum with a little water and lift the fondant onto the drum, smoothing with the fondant smoother. Use the circular cutter to cut out a series of circles from the surface and edges, and carefully remove, using the palette knife, or the cutter. Discard the cut-out circles.

2 Roll out some of the cream fondant to the same thickness as the pink fondant in step 1, and, using the same circular cutter, cut out enough circles to fill the empty spaces on the drum. Allow to set for 1 hour, and then carefully place into the circles to create a polka-dot effect. Gently smooth with the fondant smoother and set aside to harden overnight.

3 Freeze the stacked, sandwiched cakes for 1 hour. Remove from the freezer, and place on the 15cm (6in) cake board. Use a serrated knife to carve the cake into the shape of a torso, discarding any excess cake.

4 Place the sandwiched hemisphere cake (ball) on the 5cm (2in) cake board. Using the palette knife, carefully ice the surface of both cakes with buttercream and smooth (see pp182–183). Refrigerate both the cakes for 1 hour, until they set.

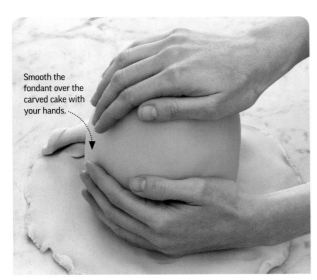

Smooth the fondant over the carved cake with your hands.

5 Dust a surface with icing sugar and roll out half the light-brown fondant to 5mm (¼in) thick, so that it is large enough to cover the carved cake. Lift over the cake and smooth. Cut off the excess fondant and tuck the edges under it. Repeat with the ball cake, tucking the edges under the board. Allow to set overnight.

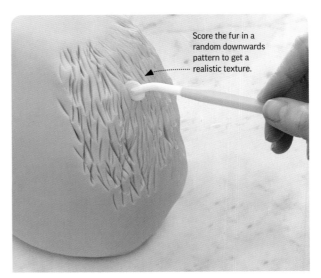

Score the fur in a random downwards pattern to get a realistic texture.

6 Use the wheel tool to score the surface of the fondant covering the torso to create the appearance of fur. Score short and long impressions in a downwards direction until the whole surface is covered. Next, score the surface of the ball cake, which will form the head.

Dowels help the
torso to support
the head.

7 Once set, insert one dowel into the centre of the torso and cut it, so that it is flush with the surface. Repeat with two more dowels, so that the torso of the teddy is stable.

8 Place the iced ball cake on the top of the bowl cake, fixing in place using royal icing. Hold until secure and allow to set for 2–3 hours.

9 While the body is setting, strengthen most of the remaining light-brown fondant (see p176) and roll four sausages to create the arms and legs. Round off both ends of each arm and then use the fondant roller to flatten one end of each, where the arm will be fixed to the torso.

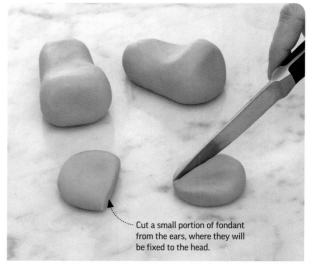

Cut a small portion of fondant from the ears, where they will be fixed to the head.

10 From the remaining two sausages, model two legs with a flat bottom for the feet. Cut the other ends into a soft diagonal, where they will be fixed to the base of the torso. Model the remaining fondant into two balls and flatten to create ears.

11 Use the wheel tool to score the surface of the arms, legs, and ears to create the appearance of fur, in the same way as the head and torso.

12 Dust a surface with icing sugar and roll out some of the remaining cream fondant to 5mm (¼in) thick and cut out an oval to form the tummy. Cut a smaller oval from the same sheet of fondant to form the muzzle.

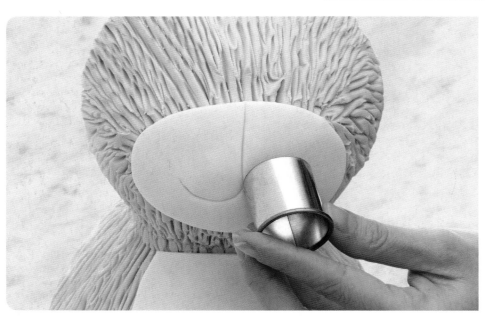

13 Move the teddy's body to the centre of the covered cake drum, using a little royal icing to secure. Fix the tummy and muzzle in place with a little water or royal icing and finish with the fondant smoother. Use the back of a knife and a circular cutter to score a smile.

Push the ball tool into the sockets lightly to create the eyes.

14 Use the ball tool to press two eye sockets into the head. Roll two small balls of strengthened black fondant and push into the sockets, fixing them in place with water. To make the nose, model the brown fondant into a soft triangle, fixing it into place at the top of the oval muzzle with a little water.

15 Dust a surface with icing sugar and roll out the remaining cream fondant to 2–3mm ($^1/_{16}$–$^1/_8$in) thick. Using the circular cutter, cut three circles. Use two circles for the feet and cut the remaining circle into half to get two semi-circles for the ears. Fix in place with a little water or royal icing and finish with the fondant smoother.

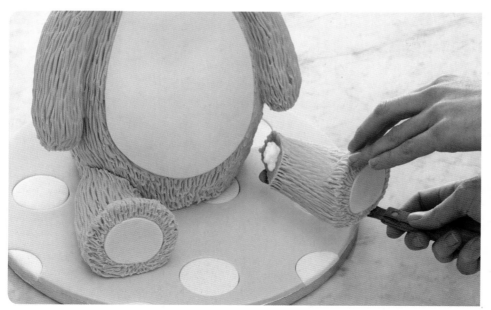

16 When the fondant limbs and body have set, apply royal icing to the inside of the arms and carefully fix them to the sides of the torso. Hold them in place with your fingers until set. To fix the legs, apply royal icing to the diagonal end of the legs. Carefully lift each leg using a palette knife and attach to the torso, holding it in place until set.

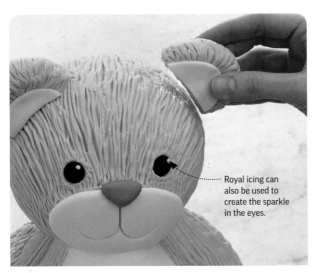

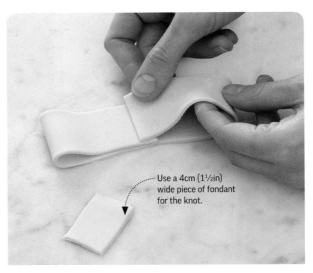

Royal icing can also be used to create the sparkle in the eyes.

Use a 4cm (1¹/₂in) wide piece of fondant for the knot.

17 Roll two tiny dots of cream fondant and fix to the eyes with a little water, to create a sparkle. To fix the ears on the teddy, apply a little royal icing to the cut edge of each ear and place on the head. Hold the ears in place with your fingers until firm.

18 To create the bow, dust a surface with icing sugar and roll out the remaining pink fondant to 3mm (¹/₈in) thick. Use the ribbon cutter to cut four strips of ribbon – three 2.5cm (1in) wide and one 4cm (1¹/₂in) wide – all about 15cm (6in) long. Fold over the wider ribbon and place the edges one over the other at the centre. Fix using a little water.

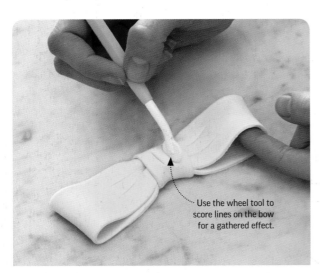

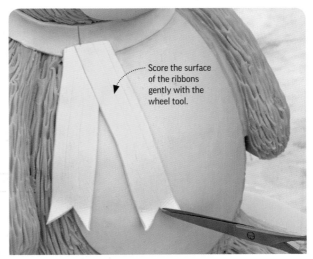

Use the wheel tool to score lines on the bow for a gathered effect.

Score the surface of the ribbons gently with the wheel tool.

19 Pinch the bow at the centre so the fondant sets into soft folds. Wrap the 4cm (1¹/₂in) fondant strip around the centre of the bow, and secure with a little water. Score with the wheel tool and set aside to dry for about 2 hours.

20 Fix one of the ribbons around the neck with water or royal icing, with the join at the front. Fix the other two ribbons together, curling them up slightly at the bottom to the centre of the collar of the teddy. Snip a small triangle from the base of both the ribbons.

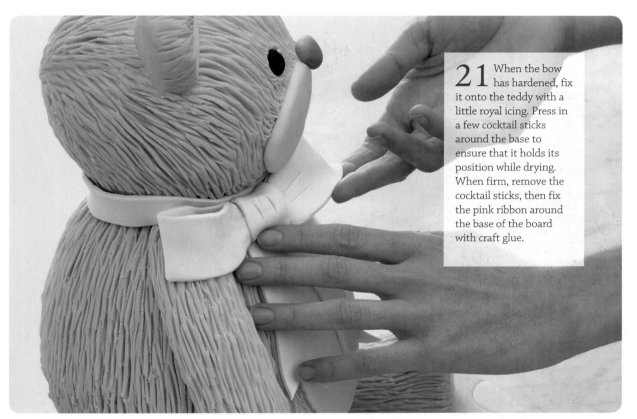

21 When the bow has hardened, fix it onto the teddy with a little royal icing. Press in a few cocktail sticks around the base to ensure that it holds its position while drying. When firm, remove the cocktail sticks, then fix the pink ribbon around the base of the board with craft glue.

Paw-print Cupcakes

Serve these gorgeous paw-print cupcakes alongside the cake or send them home with your party guests. Lightly ice the surface of cooled cupcakes (see pp174–175) with a little buttercream using a palette knife. Dust a surface with icing sugar and roll out white fondant. Use a circular cutter to create tops for the cupcakes – they should be just big enough to cover the surface of your cupcakes. Moisten the backs of the tops with a little water and fix to the cupcakes, smoothing with the fondant smoother. On a dusted surface, roll out the light-brown and pink fondants to about 3mm (¹/₈in) thick, and use circular cutters to cut three small circles and one large circle for each cupcake. Fix everything in place with a little water.

Treasure Island

With its realistic sugar sand, scary shark, cheeky crab, and treasure chest stuffed with sweets, this cake is bound to be a hit with pirate fans. The chest is made with chocolate fingers and its contents can be hand-selected. Add pirate cake pops and cupcakes to create the perfect display.

 PREP 1hr

 BAKE 25–30 mins

 DECORATE 4-5 hrs, plus overnight drying time

 SERVES 20

Ingredients

- 50g (1¾oz) dark-brown fondant, strengthened
- cornflour, for dusting
- 75g (2½oz) green flower paste (see p177)
- 100g (3½oz) grey fondant, strengthened
- 20g (¾oz) each white, black, and orange fondant, strengthened
- dry spaghetti
- 500g (1lb 2oz) royal icing, tinted sea blue, plus extra tinted green (see p181)
- 2 x 20cm (8in) square vanilla sponge cakes (see p164), sandwiched with buttercream icing (see p171)
- 250g (9oz) buttercream icing (see p180)
- 200g (7oz) light brown sugar
- icing sugar, for dusting
- 200g (7oz) green fondant, strengthened (see p176)
- 200g (7oz) dark chocolate, melted
- 20 chocolate biscuit fingers
- 100g (3½oz) yellow fondant, strengthened
- edible gold lustre dust
- rejuvenator spirit
- 50g (1¾oz) white royal icing
- mixed assorted sweets

continued overleaf...

Snip in an uneven pattern so that it resembles the bark of a coconut tree.

1 Begin by making the tree. Mould a sausage of dark-brown fondant around a cake-pop stick, so that it tapers at the top. Use scissors to snip upside-down V-shapes into the surface, to create the impression of bark. Allow to dry overnight.

2 Dust a surface with cornflour and roll out the green flower paste to 2mm (¹⁄₁₆in) thick. Use a sharp knife to cut out 6–10 leaves. Lightly score the surface using the wheel tool. To make coconuts, roll three cherry-sized balls of the dark-brown fondant and shape into ovals. Allow to dry overnight.

Equipment

- cake-pop stick, plus one stick extra (optional)
- small sewing or nail scissors
- fondant roller
- sharp knife
- wheel tool
- artists' paintbrush
- cocktail stick
- ball tool
- small circular cutter
- serrated knife
- 30cm (12in) square cake drum
- palette knife
- 3 small piping cones
- pirate flag, for decoration
- 1m (3¼ft) grey satin ribbon, 1cm (½in) wide
- craft glue

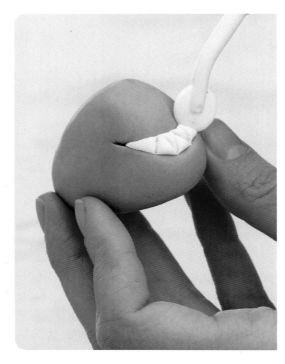

3 To make the shark, model a little of the grey fondant into a blunt cone. Cut out a wedge from the broad side for the mouth, and then smooth the edges to form a soft curve. Fit a wedge of white fondant into the mouth, fixing with water, and score teeth into the surface with the wheel tool.

4 Roll out the remaining grey fondant to 2mm (¹/₁₆in) thick and use a sharp knife to cut four gently curved fins. Poke the end of a paintbrush into the face of the shark for eye sockets, and fill with tiny balls of black fondant. Using a cocktail stick, poke two holes for the nostrils. Set it all aside to dry overnight.

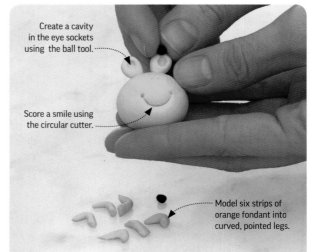

Create a cavity in the eye sockets using the ball tool.

Score a smile using the circular cutter.

Model six strips of orange fondant into curved, pointed legs.

5 For the crab, roll a cherry-sized ball of orange fondant for the head. Roll two tiny balls of the same fondant and flatten a little for eyes. Create eye sockets with the ball tool and fix two tiny balls of black fondant into the cavities with water. Make six pointed legs and fix to the body with water.

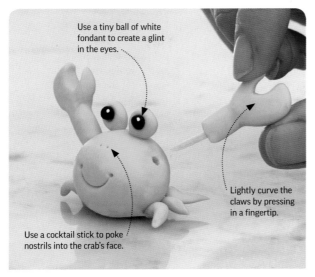

Use a tiny ball of white fondant to create a glint in the eyes.

Lightly curve the claws by pressing in a fingertip.

Use a cocktail stick to poke nostrils into the crab's face.

Make sure the leaves overlap at the tips to form a strong base.

6 To create claws, make two small sausages of orange fondant, each on a small piece of dry spaghetti. Model a small ball at the end of each, flatten with the roller, then snip out a V-shape on each using scissors. Allow to harden for 1 hour, then fix to the body using the spaghetti. Set aside to dry overnight.

7 Assemble the tree by fixing the coconuts and leaves together with the green royal icing. Hold each leaf in place, or support with folded kitchen towel, until the royal icing just begins to set.

8 Carefully place the trunk in the centre of the leaves and fix in place with the green royal icing. Hold with your fingers until firm. Allow to dry for 2–3 hours.

9 Freeze the sandwiched sponge cakes for 1 hour. Remove from the freezer, place on a sheet of greaseproof paper, and carve into a rugged island shape using a serrated knife. Discard the trimmings and crumb coat the cake with buttercream icing (see p171), then refrigerate for 30 minutes.

Score lines around the edges using the wheel tool. ⋯⋯⋯

10 Carefully lift the cake onto the cake drum, then apply a second coating of buttercream icing using the palette knife. Press the brown sugar into the buttercream so it covers the top and sides, giving the impression of sand. Allow to set for 30 minutes then brush away any excess sugar from the drum.

11 Dust a surface with icing sugar, and roll out the green fondant to about 3mm (1/8in) thick. Using a sharp knife, cut an irregular rectangle to cover the top of the island. Fix in place with water, then shape the edges into uneven scallops. Refrigerate the island until all the other cake elements are ready.

12 For the treasure chest, brush a rectangle of melted chocolate onto greaseproof paper. Place five chocolate fingers on the melted chocolate. Allow to harden and remove from the greaseproof paper. Repeat to create three more panels. Use a sharp knife to cut off any excess chocolate.

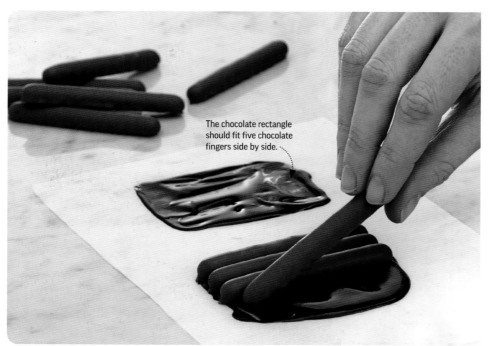

The chocolate rectangle should fit five chocolate fingers side by side. ⋯

13 Cut one panel in half to create the sides of the chest. Fill a piping cone with melted chocolate. Apply a little chocolate to the edges of the panel to assemble the chest. Set aside one panel for the lid.

Apply melted chocolate to the half panels to attach to the sides of the chest.

Piping cone

Fold a square of greaseproof paper in half to make a triangle, then in half again. Roll it over into a cone shape, and expand it out with your fingers. Fill with chocolate and snip off the end.

Fold each rectangle in an L-shape and attach to the edges of the chest.

14 Roll out the yellow fondant to about 2mm (¹⁄₁₆in) thick, and cut four rectangles. Create rivets in the rectangles with the end of a paintbrush, as shown, then fix to the chest with a little water. Mix the edible gold lustre dust with rejuvenator spirit and paint the rectangles. Set aside to dry.

15 Use a palette knife to paddle the blue royal icing over the surface of the cake drum, around the island, to create a series of waves, ensuring that the surface of the drum is covered. Smooth waves up the side of the island. Allow to set for 30 minutes.

16 Pipe white royal icing to the tips of the waves in a series of squiggles, to create whitecaps. Sprinkle a little brown sugar around the base of the island to create a beach effect.

17 Press the head of the shark into the royal icing sea and place a fin directly behind it. Fix the remaining fins into the royal icing sea around the base of the island.

Assembling

You can use green candy melts instead of royal icing to fix the leaves and trunk. Simply melt and apply with a paintbrush. Allow to harden before placing the tree on the island.

18 Set the treasure chest on top of the island. Press the tree onto the top of the cake so that the cake-pop stick supports it.

Pipe some melted chocolate to fix the half-open lid, and hold until firm.

19 Place the crab on the cake, fixing in place with a little water. Fill the treasure chest with sweets, such as, candy necklaces, gold coins, candy-coated chocolate buttons, and jelly beans, so they spill over the sides. Add a jaunty shop-bought pirate flag on top of the chest. Finally, fix the ribbon around the base of the drum with craft glue.

Cake-pop Pirates

Dip cake pops into ivory or flesh-coloured candy melts (see p173), or white chocolate, if desired. Allow to set, and melt red, green, and blue candy melts in separate bowls. Dip just the tops of the balls into the melts to create bandanas. Model ties from red, green, and blue fondant, and fix into place with a little water. Use an edible black pen to create eyes, a smile, and the stubble.

To make the nose, roll a tiny ball of flesh-coloured fondant and fix to the face with water. Roll out black fondant very thinly and cut out eye patches, fixing onto the face with water. To finish, tie matching lengths of coloured ribbons at the base of each cake pop.

Easy *animal* cakes

Simple round sponge cakes can be transformed into a virtual zoo of animals. Bake two cakes, one for the face and one to make extra legs, snouts and ears. Add coloured buttercream, some shop-bought goodies, and a little imagination for an impressive party cake. You could use any leftover cake to make some animal cake pops.

Circles of cake iced with bright-green buttercream

Liquorice wheels

Liquorice laces

White fondant

Carved cake

Jelly beans

Pale-pink fondant

Carved cake

Pale-yellow fondant

Bright-green buttercream

Friendly frog

Playful panda

- Natural buttercream
- Black buttercream
- Carved cake
- Black gummy sweets
- Carved cake
- Strawberry liquorice laces
- Black buttercream
- Black fondant

Tame tiger

- Black fondant
- Bright-orange buttercream
- Natural buttercream
- Carved cake
- Pink jelly beans
- Black liquorice laces
- Pale-pink fondant
- White marshamllows, halved, with green diamond gummy sweet

Mischievous monkey

- Chocolate buttercream
- Pale-yellow fondant
- Light chocolate buttercream
- Carved cake
- Light chocolate buttercream
- Melted milk chocolate, piped
- Giant chocolate buttons

Pretty pig

- Pink fondant triangles
- Black liquorice
- Pink fondant
- Black gummy sweets
- Circle of cake
- Pink fondant
- Bright-pink candy melts, piped

Over the Rainbow

Create this stunning rainbow cake from multi-coloured layers of sponge cake, iced with matching rows of buttercream. Place a gorgeous fondant rainbow, dusted with glitter and sitting on fluffy clouds, on top to create a perfect party centrepiece.

PREP 1½ hrs   **BAKE** 1½ hrs   **DECORATE** 2-3 hrs, plus overnight drying time   **SERVES** 20-25

Ingredients

- 25g (scant 1oz) lilac fondant, strengthened (see p176)
- 25g (scant 1oz) light-blue fondant, strengthened
- 45g (1½oz) light-green fondant, strengthened
- 45g (1½oz) yellow fondant, strengthened
- 45g (1½oz) orange fondant, strengthened
- 45g (1½oz) fuchsia fondant, strengthened
- cornflour, for dusting
- 400g (14oz) white fondant, strengthened
- 2 batches of vanilla sponge batter (see p164)
- 1¼ tsp lilac colouring paste
- 1¼ tsp turquoise colouring paste
- 1¼ tsp light-green colouring paste
- 1¼ tsp yellow colouring paste
- 1¼ tsp orange colouring paste
- 1¼ tsp pink colouring paste
- 1kg (2¼lb) vanilla buttercream icing (see p180)
- fine edible glitter

continued overleaf...

1 To make the rainbow topper, roll each of the six colours of fondant into ropes, about 5mm (¼in) wide and 15cm (6in) long. On a dusted surface, place the circular cutter, or a wide-base glass, and position the lilac rope around it in the shape of a rainbow. Brush the outside edge of the rope with a little water and carefully press the blue rope around it. Continue with all the colours, until all ropes are in position.

2 While the fondant ropes are still soft, use the sharp knife to cut the rainbow evenly across the ends, to give it a flat base. Set it aside to dry for 2 days.

Equipment

- 6cm (2½in) circular cutter
- sharp knife
- fondant roller
- 30cm (12in) cake drum
- fondant smoother
- two 20cm (8in) round cake tins
- palette knife
- large piping bag
- large piping nozzle with round tip (PME no. 18)
- 1m (3¼ft) pink satin ribbon, 1cm (½in) wide
- craft glue

3 Dust a surface with cornflour. Using the fondant roller, roll out the strengthened white fondant to about 3mm (⅛in) thick. It should be large enough to cover the cake drum. Brush the cake drum with a little water, and cover with the fondant, using the smoother to create an even surface (see p179). Trim the excess fondant using a sharp knife and wrap in cling film for later use. Set aside to dry overnight.

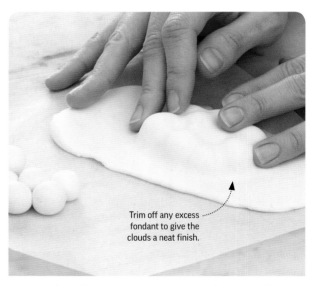

Trim off any excess fondant to give the clouds a neat finish.

4 To make the clouds, mould some of the reserved white fondant into 30 small balls, each approximately the size of a small marble, and set aside to harden for 3 hours.

5 On a dusted surface, roll out the rest of the reserved white fondant into a very thin sheet. Cut into two and press each half over 15 balls. Trim the excess and tuck the edges under the clouds. Set aside for 3 hours.

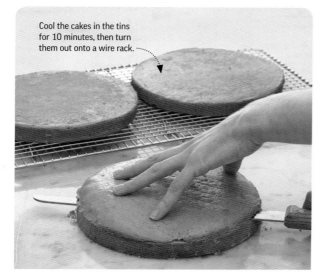

Cool the cakes in the tins for 10 minutes, then turn them out onto a wire rack.

6 Prepare the baking tins (see pp168–9). Divide the batter between six bowls, add 1 teaspoon of colouring paste to each, and blend, to get lilac, turquoise, green, yellow, orange, and pink batters. Bake for 25 minutes and leave to cool. Trim off any brown edges and level the cakes (see pp170–1).

7 Divide the buttercream icing into seven bowls and tint six of these using one of each colouring paste (see p180). Start with the lilac cake and top with lilac buttercream. Place the turquoise cake on top and smooth turquoise buttercream over it. Top with the green cake and a layer of green buttercream.

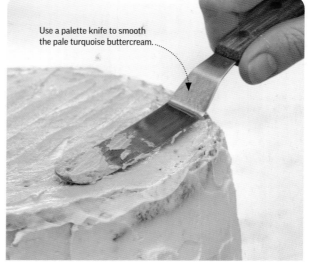

Use a palette knife to smooth the pale turquoise buttercream.

8 Continue stacking the cakes with their corresponding buttercream colours, following the image on page 60, until you finish with the pink sponge on top. Move the cake to the covered cake drum.

9 Crumb coat the entire cake (see p171) using the untinted buttercream, and refrigerate for 30–60 minutes. Add some of the untinted buttercream to the leftover turquoise buttercream and smooth over the top of the cake. Leave to set for 1 hour.

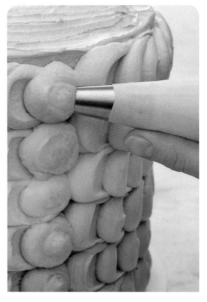

10 Fix the piping nozzle to the piping bag and fill with lilac buttercream. Carefully pipe a large dot of buttercream onto the lilac layer of the cake.

11 Dip the palette knife in a bowl of warm water and press into the dot to create a scallop. Repeat until you have created a row around the entire cake.

12 Continue with the turquoise, green, yellow, orange, and pink buttercream, until the whole cake is covered. Finish each row with a large dot, and allow to set for 1–1 1/2 hours.

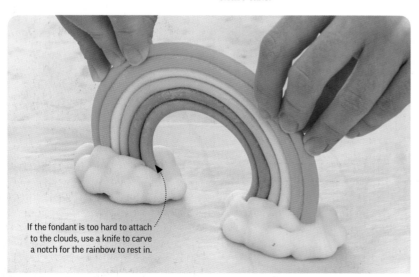

If the fondant is too hard to attach to the clouds, use a knife to carve a notch for the rainbow to rest in.

13 Attach the clouds to each end of the rainbow, using a little water to fix. Set aside to dry, until it is hard and firm enough to stand upright.

14 Once the rainbow and clouds have dried, lightly dust the surface with edible glitter to add some sparkle.

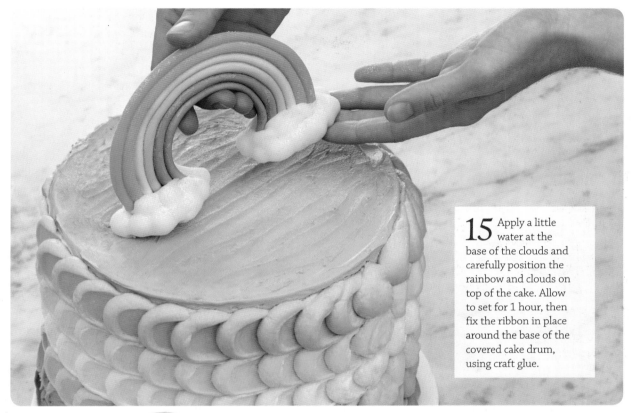

15 Apply a little water at the base of the clouds and carefully position the rainbow and clouds on top of the cake. Allow to set for 1 hour, then fix the ribbon in place around the base of the covered cake drum, using craft glue.

Pop of Colour Cupcakes

Simple cupcakes (see pp174–3), iced with pastel buttercream to match the colours of the rainbow, are a perfect addition to your party table. Pile buttercream onto the centre of each cupcake and use a palette knife to spread the icing in a generous swirl, working from the inside out. If desired, you can make mini rainbows or clouds from leftover fondant. If you lay them flat on the cupcakes, they won't need to harden first.

Party Train

Load this colourful, three-dimensional train with sweet cargo, and sit it on edible train tracks, complete with ballast. Easily carved from sponge cakes, and using shop-bought decorations, it is a show-stopper cake that will charm any child.

 PREP 1 hr   **BAKE** 40–50 mins    **DECORATE** 2½–3 hrs, plus overnight drying time   **SERVES** 20

Ingredients

- cornflour, for dusting
- 500g (1lb 2oz) green fondant, strengthened (see p186)
- 2 x 23cm (9in) square sponge cakes (see p186)
- 500g (1lb 2oz) vanilla buttercream (see p180)
- icing sugar, for dusting
- 300g (10oz) blue fondant
- 300g (10oz) red fondant
- miniature and full-sized chocolate sandwich biscuits
- 50g (1¾oz) royal icing (see p181)
- mixed sweets, including candy-coated chocolate buttons and jelly beans
- 1 miniature cupcake
- 1 large marshmallow

continued overleaf...

Candy-coated chocolate buttons make perfect accessories for the engine and carriages.

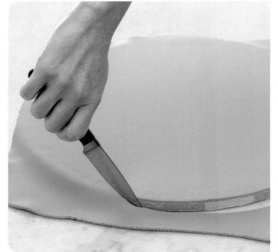

1 Dust a surface with cornflour and roll out the strengthened green fondant to about 3mm (⅛in) thick. The fondant should be large enough to cover the cake drum. Brush the cake drum with a little water, and cover with the fondant, using the fondant smoother to create an even surface. Cut off the excess using a sharp knife. Set the covered drum aside to dry overnight. Wrap the remaining green fondant in cling film and reserve for later use.

2 To create the train carriages, cut three rectangular blocks, each about 8 x 5cm (3¼ x 2in), out of one of the sponges. Place the blocks on a sheet of greaseproof paper and crumb coat each block with buttercream (see p171). Allow them to set for 1 hour.

- rectangular shortcake-style biscuits
- 200g (7oz) dark-grey fondant, strengthened
- 300g (10oz) orange fondant
- 300g (10oz) green fondant
- chocolate finger biscuits
- 200g (7oz) light-grey fondant, strengthened
- candy floss

Equipment
- fondant roller
- 35cm (14in) round cake drum
- fondant smoother
- sharp knife
- palette knife
- small artist's paintbrush
- piping bag
- 1 piping nozzle (PME no. 2)
- 1m (3¼ft) blue satin ribbon, 1cm (½ in) wide
- craft glue

Sandwich the two rectangular blocks with buttercream to make the cabin.

3 To make the engine, cut out two rectangular blocks from the other sponge cake, each about 8 x 6cm (3¼ x 2½in). Use a sharp knife to carve one of the blocks into a half cylinder to form the front section of the train and place on a sheet of greaseproof paper. Cut the remaining block in half. Fix one half to the front of the train with buttercream. Spread buttercream on top and place the second half on top. Crumb coat the whole engine with buttercream (see p171). Allow to set for 1 hour.

4 Lightly buttercream the surface of the engine. Dust a surface with icing sugar and roll out the blue fondant to about 3mm (⅛in) thick. Cover the engine with the fondant, smoothing it down with your hands, or use the smoother. Cut away the excess and tuck the edges underneath.

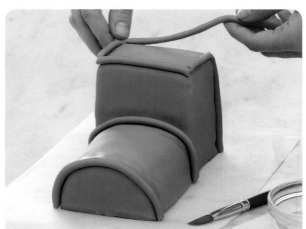

5 Roll several long, narrow ropes of some of the red fondant, about 5mm (¼in) thick. From these, cut smaller ropes to "pipe" the top of the cabin and the front of the engine. Moisten the backs of the ropes with water using a paintbrush and fix into place on the train.

 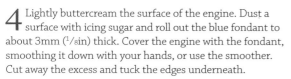

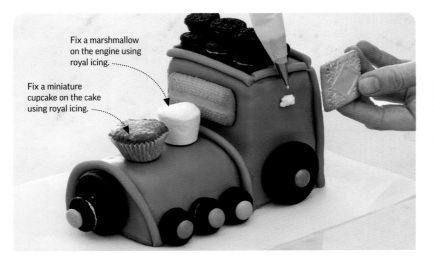

Fix a marshmallow on the engine using royal icing. ········

Fix a miniature cupcake on the cake using royal icing. ········

6 Fix miniature chocolate biscuits to each side of the engine with royal icing, to create wheels. Fix two large chocolate biscuits to make wheels for the cabin. Fix another large chocolate biscuit to the front of the train and top with a smaller one. Stick a candy-coated chocolate button to each wheel using royal icing. Glue miniature chocolate biscuits to the top of the cabin, using royal icing. Fit four shortcake-style biscuits to the front, back, and sides of the cabin, to create windows.

7 Using the strengthened dark-grey fondant, roll tiny balls to create the stones for the ballast. Set aside to harden for about 5 hours.

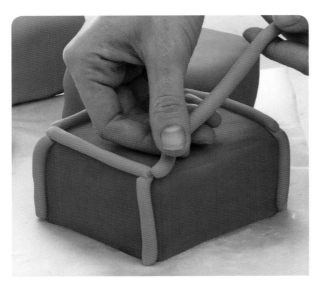

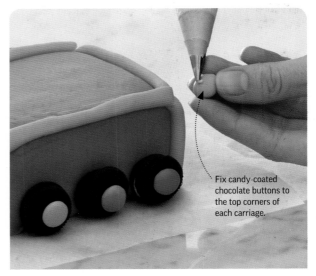

Fix candy-coated chocolate buttons to the top corners of each carriage.

8 Cover the three carriages using the red, orange, and green fondant, as in step 4. Create borders for the carriages; rolling orange ropes to pipe the red carriage, blue ropes for the green carriage, and green ropes for the orange carriage. Fix the fondant ropes in place with water.

9 Add miniature chocolate biscuits to create wheels on the sides, and top each with a candy-coated chocolate button. Add another to the front of each carriage, to create a headlight, fixing all in place with royal icing.

10 Apply a thin layer of royal icing, or edible glue, on top of each carriage. Fill the top of the orange carriage with jelly beans, the green carriage with chocolate finger biscuits, and the red carriage with candy-coated chocolate buttons – or choose your own "cargo". Place the engine and the carriages on the covered cake drum in a semicircle.

11 For the tracks, dust a surface with cornflour and roll out the light-grey fondant to 2mm ($^1/_{16}$in) thick. Cut out long ribbons to fit between the carriages and the engine, and from the ends of the train to the edge of the drum.

Using a sharp knife, cut out 5mm ($^1/_4$in) wide ribbons.

12 Moisten the backs of the ribbons with water and smooth into place on the cake drum, so that they form a gentle curve. Use the tip of the piping nozzle to emboss rivets on them.

13 Fix the chocolate finger biscuits in place between the tracks, using a little royal icing, for trestles. When the stones are dry, dab the spaces between the finger biscuits with royal icing and fill with the stones.

14 Allow the cake to set for 1 hour, and then fix the blue ribbon in place around the base of the drum, using craft glue.

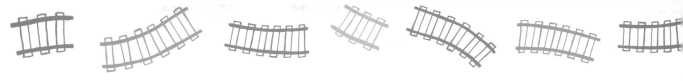

15 Pipe a peak of buttercream icing on the miniature cupcake and allow to dry. Finally, press a puff of candy floss steam into the buttercream icing.

Cargo Cupcakes

Replicate the cargo carriages of your train with sweets-topped cupcakes (see pp174–5) – perfect for party bags. Fit a large circular piping nozzle onto a large piping bag and fill with green buttercream icing. Pipe a generous swirl onto the surface of each cupcake, and then top with sweets to match your carriages – or create new cargo altogether.

Animal cake pops

No matter what your theme, an animal cake pop is bound to complete it! Model your cake pops to shape, chill, dip in candy melts, and decorate with a variety of easy-to-find ingredients and easy-to-master coating and piping techniques.

Dark chocolate, piped

Green candy melts, piped

White fondant balls

White candy melts, piped

Green candy melts

Clever croc

Light-grey candy melts

Dark chocolate, piped

Blue candy-coated chocolate sweets

Large heart-shaped sprinkle, inverted

Small heart-shaped sprinkle

Flower sprinkles

Cute owl

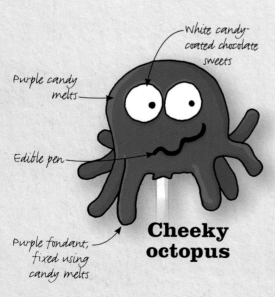

White candy-coated chocolate sweets

Purple candy melts

Edible pen

Purple fondant, fixed using candy melts

Cheeky octopus

Fondant cone covered in gold edible glitter

Pink candy melts

White/pale pink fondant

Edible pen

Various colours of food colouring paste, mixed with rejuvenator fluid and painted on

Magic unicorn

Speedy snail

Light-green candy melts

Edible pen

Round mints

Edible pen

Green candy melts

Cuddly koala

Grey fondant disc, fixed using candy melts

Black jelly bean

Edible pen

Grey candy melts

Baby dinosaur

Edible pen

Red fondant triangles

Blue candy melts

Playful puppy

White chocolate, piped

Dark chocolate, piped

Golden biscuit crumbs

Brown fondant oval

Light-brown candy melt

Pretty pufferfish

Red lustre dust

Orange candy melts

Edible pen

White candy melts, piped

Heart-shaped sprinkle, halved

Green glitter on piped green candy melts

Tropical parrot

Edible pen

Yellow fondant, fixed using candy melts

White candy melts, piped

Dark orange candy melts

Light orange candy melts

Green candy melts

Red candy melts

Animal cake pops ☆ 73

Dinosaur Egg

This baby dinosaur, with its spiked and spotted tail, just emerging from his egg, is a crowd-pleaser. The egg is made by stacking delicious sponges and wrapping in ivory fondant that is then speckled with edible paint. Get ready for some prehistoric fun.

 PREP 40-50 mins   **BAKE** 1-2 hrs   **DECORATE** 3-4 hrs, plus overnight drying time   **SERVES** 30

Ingredients

- cornflour, for dusting
- 500g (1lb 2oz) green fondant, strengthened (see p176)
- 23cm (9in) round sponge cake (see p164)
- 20cm (8in) round sponge cake
- 15cm (6in) hemisphere sponge cake (see p186)
- 500g (1lb 2oz) buttercream icing (see p180)
- icing sugar, for dusting
- 1kg (2¼lb) ivory fondant
- brown colouring paste
- rejuvenator spirit
- 300g (10oz) crisp rice bars
- white vegetable fat, for greasing
- 500g (1lb 2oz) orange fondant, strengthened
- 25g (scant 1oz) white fondant

continued overleaf...

Speckled candy-covered chocolate eggs or jelly beans are perfect additions to the theme.

1 Dust a surface with cornflour and roll out the strengthened green fondant to about 3mm (1/8in) thick, so that it is large enough to cover the cake drum. Brush the cake drum with a little water and cover with the fondant. Use the smoother to create an even surface. Cut off any excess using a sharp knife. Set the covered drum aside to dry overnight. Wrap the remaining green fondant in cling film for later use.

2 Place the 23cm (9in) sponge cake on a sheet of greaseproof paper. Using the palette knife, paddle some buttercream icing on the top and place the 20cm (8in) sponge on it. Apply some more buttercream icing on top of this cake and place the inverted bowl cake over it.

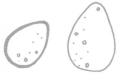
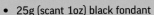

- 25g (scant 1oz) black fondant
- 100g (3½oz) blue fondant, strengthened
- 25g (scant 1oz) chocolate

Equipment

- fondant roller and smoother
- 30cm (12in) cake drum
- sharp knife
- palette knife
- serrated knife
- 1 plastic dowel
- small artist's paintbrush
- ball tool
- 2 cake-pop sticks
- cocktail sticks
- 1m (3¼ft) orange satin ribbon, 1cm (½in) wide
- craft glue

3 Using the serrated knife, carefully carve the structure from the base of the bowl cake down to the bottom of the largest sponge cake to create a smooth, even surface. Carve just enough to produce a gently curved egg shape. Use a palette knife to crumb coat the entire surface of the egg shape (see p171), and refrigerate for 30–60 minutes, until set.

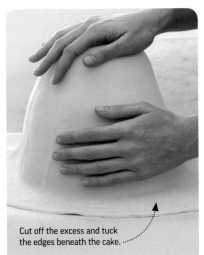

Cut off the excess and tuck the edges beneath the cake.

4 Apply a thin layer of buttercream onto the crumb-coated cake and refrigerate for a further 1 hour. When the cake has set, press the dowel through its centre to provide support.

5 Dust a surface with icing sugar and roll out the ivory fondant to about 3mm (⅛in) thick – it should be large enough to cover the entire cake. Lift the fondant over the cake and smooth down with your hands.

6 Use the sharp knife to score a jagged star shape into the surface of the top side of the cake. Cut out a similar shape at the base of the cake on the opposite side, for the tail to emerge.

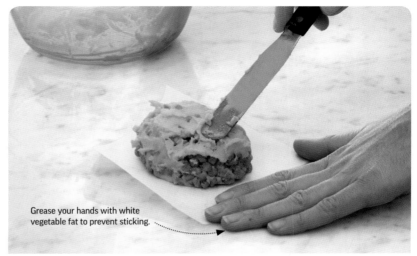

Grease your hands with white vegetable fat to prevent sticking.

7 Mix together the brown colouring paste and rejuvenator spirit. Dip the paintbrush into it and then flick towards the cake to create a speckled appearance. Set aside, ideally overnight.

8 Model about half the crisp rice bars to form the dinosaur head. Begin by creating a cone shape and then flatten slightly and round the top and bottom. Use your fingers or a ball tool to press in nostrils, eye sockets, and a slight indentation where the snout begins. Place the head on greaseproof paper, and using the palette knife, or a small spatula, lightly apply some buttercream on it. Set aside to dry.

Press the fondant into the eye sockets and nostrils.

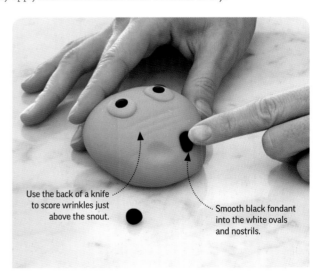

Use the back of a knife to score wrinkles just above the snout.

Smooth black fondant into the white ovals and nostrils.

9 Dust a surface with icing sugar and roll out half of the orange fondant to about 3mm (1/8in) thick. Dust your hands with icing sugar and cover the dinosaur head with fondant. Cut off any excess and tuck the edges under the back of the head, pressing the fondant together with your fingers and then smoothing with the fondant smoother.

10 Model two balls of white fondant, flatten into ovals, and fix into the eye sockets with a little water. Press the ball tool into the white ovals in the centre. Roll pea-sized balls of black fondant, moisten the backs, and press into the cavities. Model two slightly larger ovals of black fondant and fit into the nostrils, using a little water. Set aside.

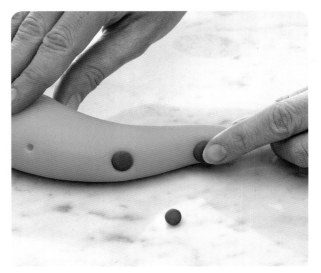

11 Form the remaining crisp rice bars into a gently curved tail – larger at one end and tapering to a point at the other end – about 18cm (7in) in length. Cover with buttercream and then with the orange fondant, as in step 9, using your hands to smooth.

12 While the fondant is still soft, use both ends of the ball tool and the end of the paintbrush to make indentations into the surface of the tail in a random pattern. Model some of the strengthened blue fondant into small balls and carefully press into the cavities, using a little water. Use the fondant smoother to achieve an even surface.

13 Dust a surface with cornflour and roll out the remaining blue fondant to about 3mm (1/8in) thick. Using a sharp knife cut out 16 spikes (14 the same size, then a larger one for the head and a smaller one for the tip of the tail).

14 Soften the edges of the spikes with your fingers so they are nicely rounded. Moisten the base of each spike with a little water, place the larger spike on the head and the remaining ones down the tail, with the smallest spike at the end.

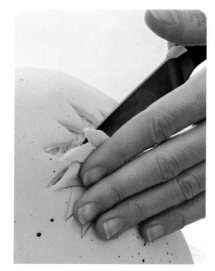

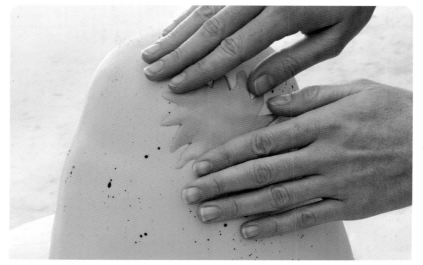

15 Cut out the jagged star shapes from the cake and, using a knife, lift away from the buttercream beneath without pulling away any of the cake. Scrape any buttercream from the back and reserve the star shapes.

16 Dust a surface with icing sugar and roll out the remaining orange fondant to 3mm (1/8in) thick. Use the ivory fondant star shapes as templates to cut two identical shapes from the orange fondant. Moisten the backs and press into the spaces on the cake. Use the ball tool to create some cavities on the surface of each star shape, fill with the blue fondant balls (see step 12), and smooth the surface.

17 Transfer the cake to the covered drum, and press the tail into place against the orange fondant. Use a little water to fix the tail in place.

Dino head

If you do not feel confident using crisp rice bars for the head and tail, you can make them entirely from fondant. Use cake-pop sticks or dowels to support the head.

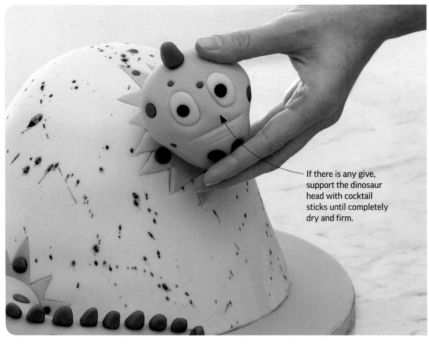

If there is any give, support the dinosaur head with cocktail sticks until completely dry and firm.

18 Melt the chocolate and dip both ends of each cake-pop stick in it, so about 2.5cm (1in) of each end is covered in chocolate. Press both the sticks down into the cake, in the centre of the orange broken eggshell shape, about 3cm (1¼in) apart. Make sure that each cake-pop stick protrudes at a slightly upwards angle from the surface to fully support the head. Spread a little chocolate on the back of the head, slip the head onto the cake-pop sticks, and press into place. Hold for 2–3 minutes, until the chocolate has hardened.

19 Cut out a small jagged star shape from the speckled shape removed from the cake in step 15. Curve over the top right of the dinosaur's head, and fix in place using water.

20 Dust a surface with icing sugar and roll out the remaining green fondant to about 2mm (¹⁄₁₆in) thick. Cut tufts of grass in random heights and shapes. Moisten the backs and fix around the base of the egg.

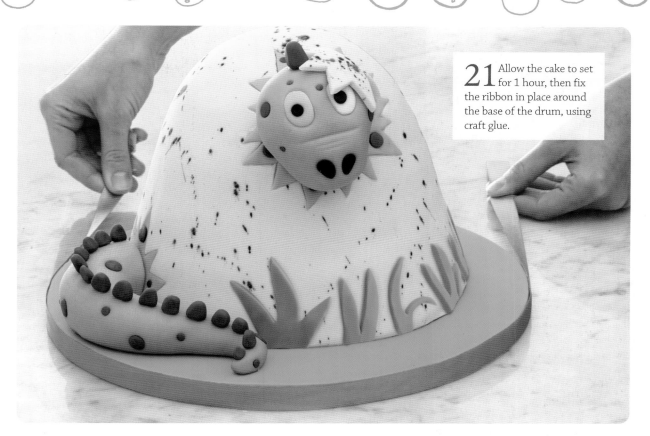

21 Allow the cake to set for 1 hour, then fix the ribbon in place around the base of the drum, using craft glue.

Dinosaur Egg Cupcakes

These delightful cupcakes are remarkably easy to make. Simply pipe or spread chocolate buttercream icing or ganache on the surface of each cupcake (see pp174–175), cover with finely grated milk or dark chocolate, and then top with speckled chocolate eggs. These cupcakes would be a great idea for Easter celebrations, too. Add a fondant tail emerging from one of the eggs, if you have got the time.

Cupcake Owl

Create this lovely owl by decorating iced cupcakes with a host of shop-bought biscuits, chocolates, and sweets. It couldn't be easier to make and will delight children with its quirky design. Party bags spilling over with chocolate "owl eggs" add to the theme.

 PREP 30 mins   **BAKE** 15 mins   **DECORATE** 30–45 mins, plus drying time   **SERVES** 16

Ingredients

- 16 vanilla sponge cupcakes in plain paper cases (see p164)
- 200g (7oz) buttercream icing, tinted yellow (see p180)
- 300g (10oz) buttercream icing, tinted sage green
- 5 chocolate-covered cake biscuits
- 200g (7oz) white chocolate buttons, reserve one to melt
- 75g packet of Japanese chocolate dipped biscuit sticks (or pretzels)
- 25g (scant 1oz) milk chocolate, grated
- 3 large milk-chocolate buttons
- 100g (3½oz) chocolate chips

Equipment

- palette knife
- small sharp knife

Chocolate buttons can be made at home with easy-to-use moulds.

1 Using the palette knife, cover the surface of six cupcakes with the yellow buttercream icing. To ensure a smooth surface, dip the knife in warm water before applying the icing. Cover the remaining 10 cupcakes with the sage-green buttercream icing. Set them aside.

2 Cut four of the chocolate-covered cake biscuits into halves, and the last biscuit into quarters. To make the beak of the owl, take one quarter of the cake biscuit and place it, chocolate-side down, on top of one of the green cupcakes. Place three white chocolate buttons beneath the biscuit so that the buttons overlap each other, fixing them in place using buttercream icing, if necessary.

3 For the claws, take two quarters of the biscuit and cut out inverted V-shapes from each. Place one claw on each of the two yellow cupcakes. Place broken biscuit sticks beneath them, to make a branch for the owl to rest on. Cover two more yellow cupcakes with broken biscuit sticks.

4 To make the body of the owl, take three green cupcakes and place white-chocolate buttons on them to cover the entire surface. Take two more green cupcakes, cover half of their surface with the white-chocolate buttons, and sprinkle grated milk chocolate on the remaining half of each.

Dot a small amount of melted white chocolate on each eye to create a glint.

5 For the wings, take four green cupcakes and press two halves of the chocolate-covered cake biscuits on one side of each cupcake, overlapping each other. Sprinkle grated chocolate on the remaining portion of each.

6 For the eyes, place a large milk-chocolate button in the centre of the remaining two yellow cupcakes. Surround the perimeter of each cupcake with chocolate chips. Using a sharp knife, cut the last milk-chocolate button in half and press onto the outside edge of each cupcake to create ears.

Cupcake Owl

7 Transfer the decorated cupcakes to a serving plate or board, or directly onto the table. Position the beak, wings, torso, claws, and the branch in four consecutive rows, as shown on page 82.

Little Owlet Cupcakes

Create individual baby owl cupcakes for party bags by icing extra cupcakes in yellow or green buttercream, and then adding detail. Cut chocolate-covered cake biscuits in half for the wings, and cut smaller V-shapes for the beaks. Create the eyes by topping white-chocolate buttons with chocolate drops and piping on a dot of royal icing. Fix them on the cupcakes with a little royal icing. Cut milk-chocolate buttons in half for the ear tufts, and grate chocolate onto the torso. Use buttercream to hold the wings, beak and ears in position.

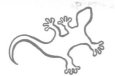

In the Jungle

Create a cast of gorgeous jungle animals set in a deep green forest. The sponge cake is iced with delicious buttercream, with hand-cut leaves, plunger-cutter flowers, twisted vines, and hand-modelled characters. Complement your jungle with a zoo of animal cupcakes.

PREP 1 hr 20 mins   **BAKE** 25-30 mins   **DECORATE** 4-5 hrs, plus overnight drying time   **SERVES** 20-30

Ingredients

- 2 x 20cm (8in) round vanilla sponge cakes (see p164), sandwiched and crumb coated with buttercream icing (see p171)
- 1.5kg (3lb 3oz) vanilla buttercream icing, tinted soft green (see p180)
- cornflour, for dusting
- icing sugar, for dusting
- 25g (scant 1oz) black fondant (see p176)
- dry spaghetti
- 25g (scant 1oz) royal icing
- 25g (scant 1oz) white fondant, strengthened
- brown food colouring paste
- edible pink dust
- rejuvenator fluid

For the forest

- 200g (7oz) dark-brown fondant, strengthened
- 500g (1lb 2oz) dark-green fondant, strengthened
- 250g (9oz) medium-green fondant, strengthened
- 50g (1¾oz) light-brown fondant, strengthened
- 25g (scant 1oz) orange fondant, strengthened
- 25g (scant 1oz) pink fondant, strengthened

continued overleaf...

1 Place the cake on the cake drum. Using the palette knife, cover the cake with buttercream icing, spreading it all the way to the edges of the drum. Use a side scraper to achieve a completely smooth surface, or go around the cake with the edge of the palette knife to achieve a smooth finish.

2 To create a grassy texture, use a closed-star piping nozzle tip to score the buttercream icing. Set aside overnight to harden.

Use the knife to cut out branches.

Flatten the branches lightly with the fondant roller.

Score lightly with a knife to create the impression of bark.

3 For the trees, form seven sausages with the dark-brown fondant. They should taper at one end and be tall enough to reach the top of the cake.

- 25g (scant 1oz) yellow fondant, strengthened
- 25g (scant 1oz) purple fondant, strengthened

For the lion
- 66g (2¼oz) light-brown fondant, strengthened
- 25g (scant 1oz) white fondant
- 10g (¼oz) dark-brown fondant, strengthened
- 20g (¾oz) medium-brown fondant, strengthened

For the giraffe
- 100g (3½oz) yellow fondant, strengthened
- 10g (¼oz) dark-brown fondant, strengthened, for the horns
- 20g (¾oz) medium-brown fondant, strengthened

For the snake
- 50g (1¾oz) pale-green fondant, strengthened

For the monkey
- 35g (1¼oz) dark-brown fondant, strengthened
- 20g (¾oz) beige fondant, strengthened

For the elephant
- 75g (2½oz) light-grey fondant, strengthened
- 25g (scant 1oz) flesh-coloured fondant, strengthened

Equipment
- palette knife
- 25cm (10in) round cake drum

continued...

Cut large cloud shapes to form the tops of the trees.

Fix smaller cloud shapes to the branches.

4 Dust a surface with cornflour, roll out half the dark-green fondant to 3mm (⅛in) thick and use a sharp knife to cut seven large cloud shapes in varying sizes, and about nine smaller cloud shapes. Leave to set for 30 minutes. Roll out the remaining dark-green and half the medium-green fondant. Cut about nine large- and medium-sized clouds from each, cut each in half, and set these aside to dry overnight.

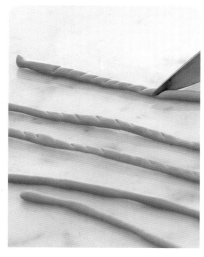

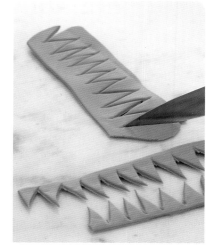

5 To make the vines, dust a surface with icing sugar and roll out eight thin ropes of the light-brown fondant. Score each rope lightly with a knife to create a vine-like effect. Set aside.

6 Roll out the remaining medium-green fondant to 2mm (¹⁄₁₆in) thick, and cut into 30, 8–10cm (3¼–4in) long strips. Using a sharp knife, cut an uneven zig-zag pattern throughout to create the appearance of grass.

- side scraper (optional)
- closed-star piping nozzle (PME no. 8)
- sharp knife
- fondant roller
- small blossom plunger cutters
- ball tool
- Dresden tool
- cocktail stick
- wheel tool
- cake-pop stick
- drinking straw, or modelling tool
- heart-shaped cutter
- 1cm (½in) circular cutters
- small scissors
- small paintbrush
- small round-tip piping nozzle
- 1m (3¼ft) green satin ribbon, 1cm (½in) wide
- craft glue

7 Roll 20 of the grass strips along the edges to create tufts of grass. Pinch together the ends with a little water to secure.

8 To make the flowers, roll out a little of the orange, pink, yellow, and purple fondants very thinly, and use the plunger cutters to cut 10–12 flowers of each colour. Use the ball tool to curve them slightly. Dry for 30 minutes.

9 Fix the trees around the cake at even intervals using a little water. Fix the vines to the cake in swags between the trees and hanging down from the branches. Moisten the bases of the half clouds and press them into the surface of the cake until the top of the cake is covered, so that they rise in an uneven pattern and resemble treetop cover.

Pinch together the points of each blade to shape, as you go.

10 Moisten the back of the remaining strips of grass with water and fix around the base of the cake. Fix the flowers to the cake in a random pattern above the grass line.

11 Moisten the base of each tuft of grass with water and press into the buttercream on the drum. Make sure you leave enough space to place the animals later.

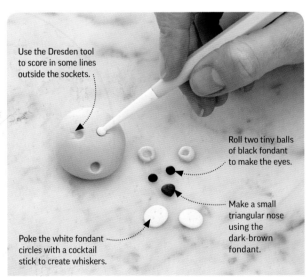

Use the Dresden tool to score in some lines outside the sockets.

Roll two tiny balls of black fondant to make the eyes.

Make a small triangular nose using the dark-brown fondant.

Poke the white fondant circles with a cocktail stick to create whiskers.

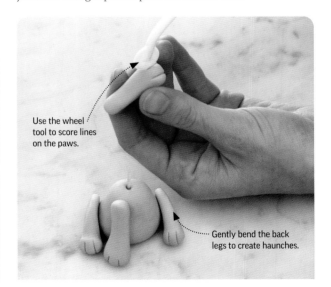

Use the wheel tool to score lines on the paws.

Gently bend the back legs to create haunches.

12 For the lion, roll a walnut-sized ball of the light-brown fondant to form the head. Roll two more small balls of the light-brown fondant, flatten them, and pinch them at the base to make ears. Use the smallest end of the ball tool to make the eye sockets and the mouth. Roll out two pea-sized balls of white fondant for the muzzle, flatten, and set aside.

13 Model a walnut-sized ball of light-brown fondant into a soft egg shape and flatten the bottom. Insert a piece of dry spaghetti into it to attach the head later. Create two front legs from small sausages of fondant with soft round paws that taper up the legs to become narrow at the top. Create a second set for the back legs and fix to the body with water.

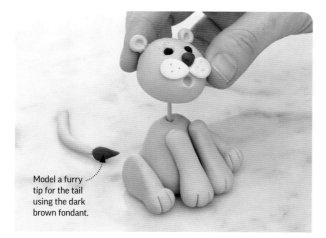

Model a furry tip for the tail using the dark brown fondant.

Place a dot of white fondant on the eyes to create a glint.

14 Place the black fondant eyes into the eye sockets and glue the ears to the head with royal icing. Fix the nose and muzzle on the face, then fix the head to the body on the spaghetti. Use the light-brown fondant to roll a thin tail.

15 Fix the tail to the body with a little water. Roll out a long strip of medium-brown fondant, about 2mm (1/16in) thick. Use the wheel tool to cut the mane out of it and then score the fur. Leave some of the scored fondant aside for a tuft of hair.

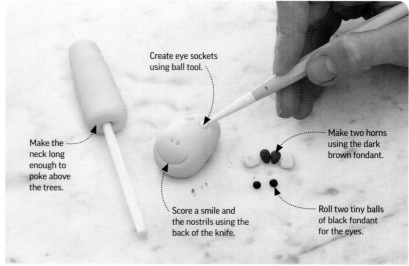

Create eye sockets using ball tool.

Make the neck long enough to poke above the trees.

Make two horns using the dark brown fondant.

Score a smile and the nostrils using the back of the knife.

Roll two tiny balls of black fondant for the eyes.

16 Apply royal icing to the edge of the mane and fix to the head. Roll the leftover fondant strip to form a tuft of mane and fix to the top of the forehead using a little royal icing. Set aside to dry overnight.

17 To make the giraffe, model some of the yellow fondant around a cake-pop stick to form the neck. Leave the other end of the cake-pop stick sticking out of the bottom. Mould a ball of yellow fondant into a gently curved, slightly flattened egg shape for the head. To make the ears, roll out a little yellow fondant, very thinly, and cut two teardrop shapes. Pinch them at the base and fix to the head using a little royal icing.

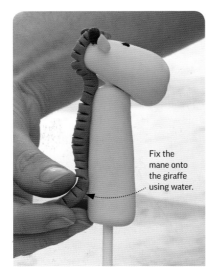

Fix the mane onto the giraffe using water.

Mix brown food colouring paste with rejuvenator spirit to create edible paint.

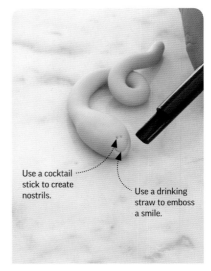

Use a cocktail stick to create nostrils.

Use a drinking straw to emboss a smile.

18 Place the eyes into the sockets and fix the ears and horns on the head using royal icing. Attach the head to the neck with royal icing. Create a mane using the medium-brown fondant.

19 Place tiny dots of royal icing or white fondant in the eyes to create a glint. Use the edible brown colour to paint markings on the giraffe. Set aside to dry overnight.

20 To make the snake, roll a sausage of pale-green fondant and use your fingers to mould a head at one end and taper the other end to a point. Curve the body into a spiral.

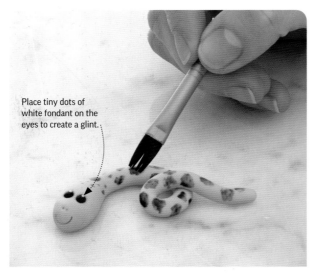

Place tiny dots of white fondant on the eyes to create a glint.

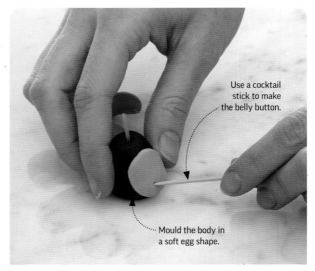

Use a cocktail stick to make the belly button.

Mould the body in a soft egg shape.

21 To make the eyes, use the ball tool to create sockets and place tiny balls of black fondant into them. Paint on the markings using the edible brown colour. Set aside to dry overnight.

22 For the monkey, roll a walnut-sized ball of dark-brown fondant. Insert a piece of dry spaghetti, with enough sticking above the the body to support the head. Dust a surface with cornflour and roll out some beige fondant thinly. Cut out an oval and fix on the torso, using a little water.

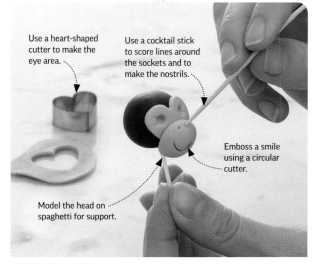

Use a heart-shaped cutter to make the eye area.

Use a cocktail stick to score lines around the sockets and to make the nostrils.

Emboss a smile using a circular cutter.

Model the head on spaghetti for support.

23 For the head, roll a small ball of dark brown fondant. On a dusted surface, roll out some beige fondant and cut out the eye area. Roll a small ball of the beige fondant and flatten to make the muzzle. Fix to the face with water. Use the ball tool to create eye sockets.

Roll two tiny balls of black fondant and place into the sockets.

24 Mix a little rejuvenator fluid to the edible pink dust and paint on the inside of the mouth. To make the ears, press two pea-sized balls of the dark brown fondant into flat circles, and then pinch the base together to cup them. Fix them to the head using a little water.

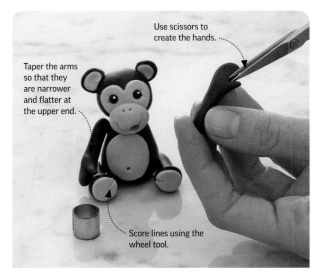

Use scissors to create the hands.

Taper the arms so that they are narrower and flatter at the upper end.

Score lines using the wheel tool.

25 Roll four small sausages of dark brown fondant for the arms and legs. Flatten the legs at the ends and dry for 1 hour. Cut four small circles of the beige fondant and fix inside the ears and at the bottom of the legs with water. Fix the limbs to the body with royal icing and set aside to dry overnight.

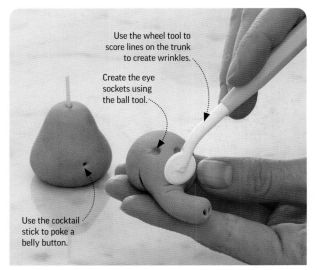

Use the wheel tool to score lines on the trunk to create wrinkles.

Create the eye sockets using the ball tool.

Use the cocktail stick to poke a belly button.

26 For the elephant, roll a ball of pale-grey fondant into a pear shape and insert a piece of dry spaghetti into it. Roll another ball of the same size, moulding some of the fondant into a sausage on one side to create a trunk. Poke two holes in the trunk with the end of a paintbrush.

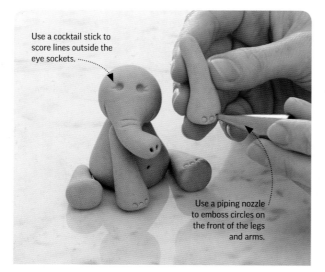

Use a cocktail stick to score lines outside the eye sockets.

Use a piping nozzle to emboss circles on the front of the legs and arms.

Place two tiny balls of black fondant into the sockets.

Place two tiny dots of white fondant on the eyes to create a glint.

Squash the ears slightly to give an oval, curved appearance.

27 Roll out two sausages to create the arms, tapering at the top, and flatten the bottom. Fix in place with some royal icing. Repeat for the legs and fix to the sides of the torso. Roll out two thick circles of grey fondant for the ears and use the ball tool to create a shallow cavity in the centre of each.

28 Emboss a mouth using the back of a small knife. Roll out a little flesh-coloured fondant thinly and cut out circles to fit the cavity in the ears. Moisten the back with water and press into place. Spread a little royal icing on the edge of each ear and fix to the head. Set aside to dry overnight.

29 Using the craft glue, fix the green satin ribbon around the base of the cake drum to give a neat finish. Place the lion on the cake. Place the snake on the top of the cake, in between the treetops.

30 Finally, place the elephant and the monkey on the cake drum and insert the giraffe into the centre of the cake.

Animal Cupcakes

Create some lovely jungle-inspired cupcakes (see pp174–5) by piping green-tinted buttercream icing through a "grass" piping nozzle. Circles of leftover fondant can be used to make tiger, hippo, and giraffe faces. Roll the fondant very thinly, and use circular cutters in a variety of sizes to produce eyes, muzzles, and ears. Mix a little brown colouring paste with rejuvenator spirit to paint on whiskers and spots, and assemble using a little water, before placing on the piped cupcakes.

Use a wide-tipped brush to stipple markings on the animals.

You can use bright fondants to create different animal faces.

Football Mania

This is a remarkably simple cake to make, and the scarf can be adjusted to match the colours of your child's favourite team. With its bright green fondant-covered cake drum and strands of fondant grass dotted around the sides, it is the ideal cake for football fans of any age.

 PREP 1 hr   **BAKE** 35–45 mins   **DECORATE** 2 hrs, plus overnight drying time   **SERVES** 10-15

Ingredients

- cornflour, for dusting
- 500g (1lb 2oz) green fondant, strengthened (see p176)
- 20cm (8in) hemisphere cake (baked in a specialty tin or an ovenproof bowl), cut in half horizontally, sandwiched with buttercream, and crumb coated (see p171)
- 200g (7oz) buttercream icing (see p180)
- icing sugar, for dusting
- 250g (9oz) white fondant
- 150g (5½oz) black fondant
- 500g (1lb 2oz) red fondant
- 300g (10oz) blue fondant

Equipment

- fondant roller
- 30cm (12in) round cake drum
- fondant smoother
- sharp knife
- palette knife
- large hexagon cutter (Tinkertech no. 959) (see p187 for template)
- large pentagon cutter (Tinkertech no. 962) (see p187 for template)
- pizza cutter (optional)
- 1m (3¼ft) blue satin ribbon, 1cm (½in) wide
- craft glue

1 Dust a surface with cornflour and roll out the strengthened green fondant to about 3mm (⅛in) thick. It should be large enough to cover the entire cake drum. Brush the drum with a little water and cover with the fondant, using the smoother to create an even surface. Cut off the excess using a sharp knife. Set aside to dry overnight. Wrap the remaining green fondant in cling film for later use.

2 Place the crumb-coated cake on a sheet of greaseproof paper. Lightly cover the surface with a thin layer of buttercream icing, using the palette knife to make it as smooth as possible.

3 Dust a surface with icing sugar, roll out the white fondant to about 3mm ($^1/_8$in) thick, and cut out 10–15 hexagons, using the hexagon cutter (see p187 for template). Cover the excess fondant in cling film and set aside for later use.

4 On the dusted surface, roll out the black fondant to about 3mm ($^1/_8$in) thick and cut out 5–10 pentagons, using the pentagon cutter (see p187 for template). Wrap the excess black fondant in cling film and set aside for later use.

Position the black pentagon carefully in the centre.

5 Brush the back of a black pentagon with a little water and place it on the top of the cake. Brush the backs of the white hexagons with water, one at a time, and carefully press them into place around the pentagon, so that the edges are flush where they meet and the surface is smooth.

6 Roll out more hexagons and pentagons, if needed, and add them to the surface of the ball to create the classic football pattern. Build up the shapes to cover the whole surface. When you reach the base, cut off any excess and smooth with the fondant smoother. Allow to set overnight.

98 Football Mania

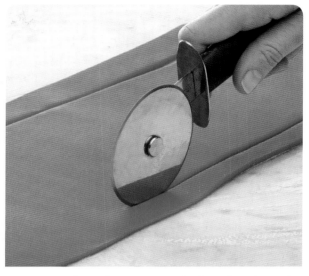

7 When the cake has set, move it to the centre of the covered drum using a palette knife.

8 Dust a surface with icing sugar and roll out the red fondant (or a fondant to match your child's team colours) to about 3mm (¹/₈in) thick. Use a pizza cutter, or a sharp knife, to cut a rectangular strip, about 36 x 6cm (14 x 2¹/₂in).

Roll out the fondant on a surface dusted with icing sugar.

9 Brush water all around the lower side of the cake, to the height of about 6cm (2¹/₂in) up from the drum. Carefully wrap the red fondant strip around the cake so that it meets at the front. Fold the extra length back on itself and fix in place with a little water.

10 Roll out some of the blue fondant to 3mm (¹/₈in) thick. Using a pizza cutter, cut a rectangular strip, 36 x 6cm (14 x 2¹/₂in). Cut this further into 7–8 rectangles, 4cm (1¹/₂in) wide.

Football Mania 99

Use a knife to cut strips through the rectangle, leaving a 1cm (½in) strip margin.

11 Brush the backs of the blue strips with a little water and place them, one by one, on the red fondant scarf at regular intervals.

12 While the fondant is soft, use a sharp knife to score little sideways Vs into the surface of the scarf, to create the appearance of knitting stitches. Continue until the whole scarf is scored.

13 Dust a surface with icing sugar and roll out the remaining blue fondant to about 3mm (¹⁄₈in) thick. Cut a rectangle, about 6 x 5cm (2¹⁄₂ x 2in) to create the end of the scarf.

14 Score the end of the blue fondant strip with Vs, brush the back with a little water, and carefully fix to the end of the folded-over red scarf.

15 Dust a surface with icing sugar, roll out the remaining green fondant to 3mm (¹⁄₈in) thick, and cut out tufts of grass with a knife.

16 Brush the backs of the tufts with water and fix around the base of the scarf in an uneven pattern.

17 Fix the blue ribbon in place around the base of the cake drum with a little craft glue.

Cake-pop Sports Balls

Create these fabulous sporty cake pops (see pp172–3) to accompany your cake. For the baseball cake pop, dip the pop in melted white candy melts and pipe on red royal icing, using a small star tip. For the tennis ball, dip the cake pop in pale yellow candy melts and pipe white royal icing. For the basketball, cover in orange candy melts and pipe black royal icing from top to base around the pop, to form seams. For the football, dip the pop in white candy melts, allow to dry, and mark the pattern using an edible black pen.

Animal cupcakes

Create a menagerie of animal cupcakes using these quirky and creative decoration ideas. You can use your child's favourite sweets to re-create their favourite animal in cupcake form.

White chocolate chips

White mini marshmallows

Brown fondant

Black writing icing

Fluffy sheep

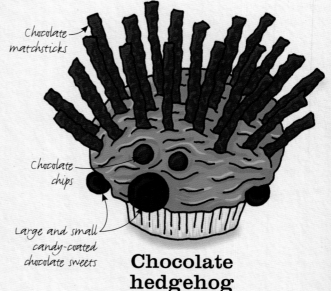

Chocolate matchsticks

Chocolate chips

Large and small candy-coated chocolate sweets

Chocolate hedgehog

Chocolate sugar strands

Yellow candy-coated chocolate sweets

Black liquorice

Triangle chocolate bar segment

Pink jelly bean

Red and black liquorice laces

Bright-eyed cat

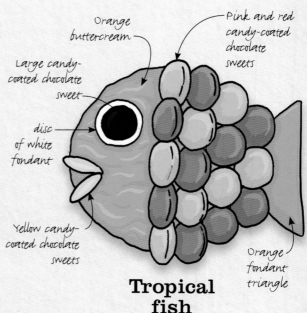

Orange buttercream

Large candy-coated chocolate sweet

disc of white fondant

Pink and red candy-coated chocolate sweets

Yellow candy-coated chocolate sweets

Orange fondant triangle

Tropical fish

Red and orange
jelly beans

Chocolate
chips

Yellow
candy-coated
chocolate sweet

Natural
buttercream

**Chirpy
chicken**

Pink
buttercream
with pink
sugar crystals
on top

Large flattened white
marshmallows, trimmed
into shape

Pale green
candy-coated
chocolate sweets

strawberry
liquorice laces

Strawberry
bon bon

Pink mini
marshmallows

**Cuddly
rabbit**

Large flattened
white marshmallows,
trimmed into
ear shape

Pink fondant

Blackcurrant
gummy sweets

Desiccated
coconut

Blackcurrant
diamond-shaped
gummy sweet,
halved

Pink fondant

**Loveable
dog**

Large white
marshmallows,
halved

Chocolate
chips

strawberry
liquorice laces

Bright green
buttercream

Crazy frog

Yellow
buttercream

Chocolate
chips

Multigrain
cereal hoops

Caramel-coated
popcorn

Blackcurrant
jelly bean

Pretzel
sticks

Black liquorice
laces

**Friendly
lion**

Prima Ballerina

This delightful ballet cake is lightly iced with buttercream, wrapped in white fondant, and adorned with satin ribbons held in place with royal icing. The beautiful ballerina is hand-modelled and held in position with spaghetti. Piping buttercream ruffles on the board means you won't need to cover it.

 PREP 50-60 mins   **BAKE** 25-30 mins   **DECORATE** 3¾ hrs, plus overnight drying time   **SERVES** 20

Ingredients

- 2 x 20cm (8in) round vanilla sponge cakes (see p164)
- 200g (7oz) vanilla buttercream icing (see p180)
- icing sugar, for dusting
- 1kg (2¼lb) white fondant (see p176)
- 500g (1lb 2oz) pale pink buttercream icing

For the ballerina
- 50g (1¾oz) flesh-coloured fondant, strengthened
- edible black pen
- edible pink dust
- 25g (scant 1oz) brown fondant, strengthened
- dry spaghetti
- 25g (scant 1oz) white fondant, strengthened
- rejuvenator spirit
- 5 tbsp royal icing
- 50g (1¾oz) pink fondant, strengthened

Equipment

- 25cm (10in) round cake drum
- fondant roller
- 2 fondant smoothers
- sharp knife
- small artist's paintbrush
- 50cm x 3mm (20in x ⅛in) pink satin ribbon

continued overleaf...

1 Sandwich and crumb coat the cakes with vanilla buttercream icing (see p171). Place them in the fridge and allow to firm for 30 minutes. Remove from the fridge and carefully place on the centre of a cake drum, using a spoonful of buttercream icing on the cake drum to fix the cake in place. Lightly ice with another layer of buttercream.

2 Dust a surface with icing sugar, and roll out the white fondant to about 5mm (¼in) thick in a circle large enough to cover the cake. Carefully lift the fondant over the top of the cake and smooth down the sides using a fondant smoother (see p178). Trim the excess fondant with a sharp knife and leave to set overnight.

- 80 x 7cm (30⅛ x 2¾in) fine pink net
- needle and pink thread
- piping nozzle (PME no. 1)
- petal piping nozzle (PME no. 57)
- piping bag
- 3m (9¾ft) pink satin ribbon, 2cm (¾in) wide
- 1m (3¼ft) pink satin ribbon, 3cm (1¼in) wide
- craft glue

Ballerina hair

For individual strands of hair, press brown fondant through a clean garlic press to create strands of hair. Fix them to the head with water while they are still moist.

3 Use two smoothers – one on the top and one on the side – to get a crisp edge at the top. Smooth in a downward motion to ensure that any trapped air bubbles are released at the base of the cake. Press the two smoothers together at the edges of the cake to get a neat line.

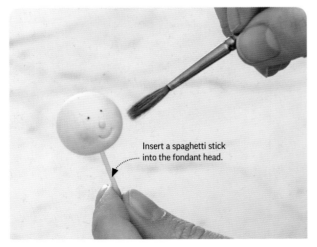

Insert a spaghetti stick into the fondant head.

4 To make the ballerina, form a cherry-sized ball from the flesh-coloured fondant for the head. Make a tiny nose from the fondant and place on the face. Emboss a mouth with the tip of a piping nozzle and mark two eyes using the edible black pen. Brush the cheeks with the edible pink dust and set aside.

5 Roll strengthened brown fondant to create strands of hair, and fix with a little water to the ballerina's head around the face. Roll a few strands of fondant into a bun and attach to the back of the head.

6 Take two lengths of spaghetti, and model two slender legs around them using a small amount of white fondant, with feet *en pointe* (on the tips of the toes). Ensure that about 5cm (2in) spaghetti extends from both ends, to insert into the cake.

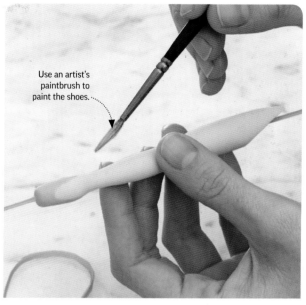

Use an artist's paintbrush to paint the shoes.

7 Mix together a little pink dust with the rejuvenator spirit and paint on the ballet shoes. Use the 3mm ($1/8$in) pink ribbon for the laces criss-crossing halfway up the calves, fixing in place with royal icing. Set aside to dry, ideally overnight.

Snip the chest area flat so that the neck will fit on.

8 Use a walnut-sized ball of strengthened pink fondant to create a slender torso and hips. Form the neck and upper torso using a small amount of the flesh-coloured fondant. Use a strand of dry spaghetti to poke a hole where the legs will fit later. Set aside to dry, ideally overnight.

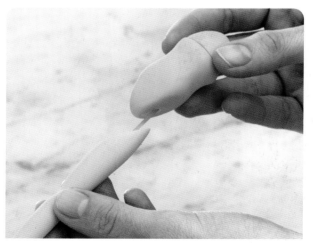

9 Once the torso is dry, carefully fix the legs by slipping the lengths of spaghetti into the torso. Moisten the top of the legs to make sure they stick.

10 Form two elegant arms from a small ball of the flesh-coloured fondant, using fine scissors to create fingers. Shape the arms so that they can be fixed onto the torso upright, in a classic *en haut* (over the head) position. Set aside to dry, ideally overnight.

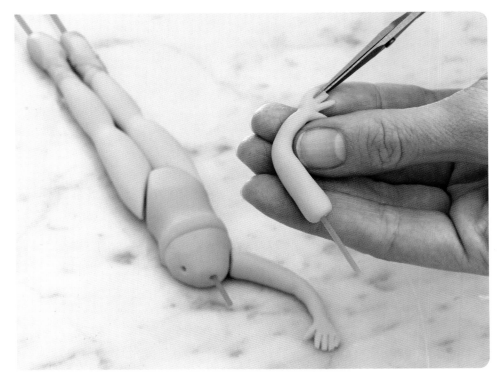

11 Fold the pink net in half lengthways, then gather it in concertina. String the concertina together using a needle and thread, to create a tutu. Leave enough thread at both ends to tie the tutu to the ballerina once she is dry. The tutu should be just long enough to fit around the waist of the ballerina.

12 Roll a long, thin rope of pink fondant and cut into six short lengths. Fix one around the bun and two as shoulder straps. Flatten one slightly to form a band around the top of the bodice. Roll the remaining two into tiny roses, one for the bodice and one for the bun, and fix in place with a little water.

13 Once the ballerina is dry, and all of the elements are secure, lay the ballerina on her front and place the tutu around her waist. Use the thread to draw the ends of the tutu together, and trim any excess netting. Tie the tutu in place, around her waist, using the excess threads, snipping stray threads with sharp scissors.

14 Attach the round piping nozzle to a piping bag and fill with royal icing. Cut two lengths of the 2cm (³/₄in) wide ribbon, each long enough to wrap once around the cake. Pipe tiny dots of royal icing to glue the ribbon to the cake. Fix one ribbon at the base of the cake and one at the top, wrapping them in a criss-cross pattern and bringing together at the front. Create a large bow with the 3cm (1¹/₄in) wide ribbon, and fix it just above the meeting of the bands with a little royal icing.

15 Attach the petal nozzle to a piping bag and fill with the buttercream icing. Working your way around the cake board, from the outer edge of the board inwards, pipe three rows of ruffles, one row at a time, to create the impression of a frilled skirt. Cover all available space on the board.

The fondant should be firm to touch.

Ruffles

To achieve even ruffles, squeeze out a length of buttercream and fold it back over itself. Apply firm pressure as you pipe the buttercream around the cake.

Ruffles should be piped close together.

Ballet Shoe Cupcakes

Spread a little buttercream icing on the top of the cupcakes (see pp174–5), and cover with a disc of white fondant, rolled to about 5mm (¼in) thick. Set aside. Use a fondant smoother to give them a polished finish.

Use strengthened pink fondant to hand-model tiny ballet shoes (one per cupcake), using the small end of the ball tool to create a cavity. Use sharp scissors to cut ribbons about 5cm (2in) long. Create slots for the ribbons on the sides of each shoe with a knife, and press the end of a length of ribbon into each. Use a knife to emboss a line around the opening of the shoes. Fix to the top of the cupcakes with a little royal icing, and allow to dry for 1 hour before displaying.

Press the tip of a small piping nozzle to create the loops of a bow.

Score in the ribbons using a sharp knife.

16 Loop the 1.5cm (¾in) wide ribbon around the base of the drum, and fix with a little craft glue. Set aside to dry. Carefully fix the ballerina to the top of the cake, pushing the spaghetti into the surface to provide support – a dot of royal icing under her feet will help to keep her in place.

Fish Tank Friends

Capture the seaside in a fish tank, with this simple, buttercream-covered sponge cake, cut to shape, iced, and decorated with frosted jelly sweets and colourful fondant fish and sea creatures. Gorgeous crab and starfish cupcakes on the side complete this aquatic theme.

 PREP 1 hr   **BAKE** 35-45 mins   **DECORATE** 3-4 hrs, plus overnight drying time   **SERVES** 25

Ingredients

- cornflour, for dusting
- 400g (14oz) pale-blue fondant, strengthened (see p176)
- 100g (3½oz) orange fondant, strengthened
- 25g (scant 1oz) white fondant, strengthened
- 25g (scant 1oz) black fondant, strengthened
- 50g (1¾oz) red fondant, strengthened
- 50g (1¾oz) lilac fondant, strengthened
- 50g (1¾oz) aqua fondant, strengthened
- 25g (scant 1oz) yellow fondant, strengthened
- 2 x 20cm (8in) square sponge cakes (see p164), cut in half, sandwiched with buttercream and crumb coated (see p171)
- 600g (1lb 5oz) buttercream icing (see p180)
- aqua colouring paste
- brown colouring paste
- edible gold glitter, or 50g (1¾oz) soft light brown sugar
- frosted jelly laces, green and red

Equipment

- fondant roller and smoother

continued overleaf...

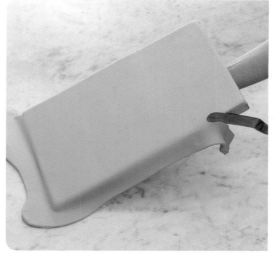

1 Dust a surface with cornflour and roll out the pale-blue fondant to about 3mm (⅛in) thick. It should be large enough to cover the cake drum. Moisten the drum with a little water and cover with the fondant, using the fondant smoother to achieve a perfect finish (see p179). Trim off the excess, cover with cling film, and set aside for later use. Allow the cake drum to dry overnight.

2 To make the fish, roll orange fondant into a cherry-sized ball and flatten with your hands to make the body. Roll a small ball of white fondant, flatten slightly, top with a tiny dot of black fondant, and place on the head to make the eyes. Roll another ball of orange fondant and model into a tail. Make different kinds of fish in varying sizes using red and lilac fondants. Make a larger goldfish tail for the top of the cake. Set everything aside to dry overnight.

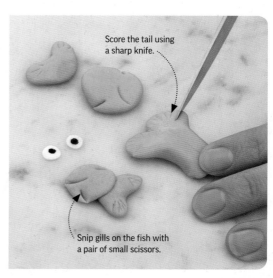

Score the tail using a sharp knife.

Snip gills on the fish with a pair of small scissors.

- 30 x 20cm (12 x 8in) rectangular cake drum
- sharp knife
- small scissors
- star cutter
- piping nozzle (PME no. 2)
- palette knife
- 1m (3¼ft) blue satin ribbon, 1cm (½in) wide
- craft glue

Marbling

Mix a little red fondant with a tiny ball of white fondant and blend to get a marbled effect. Use the two-toned fondant to create fish, as shown in step 2.

3 To make the seaweed, dust a surface with cornflour, roll out the aqua fondant to about 2mm (¹/₁₆in) thick, and cut thin ribbons. Holding the ends of one ribbon at a time, twist, and set aside to dry for 1 day.

Gently emboss the surface using the tip of a piping nozzle.

Create curved upward tips with your fingers.

4 For the starfish, dust a surface with cornflour and roll out the remaining lilac fondant to about 2–3mm (¹/₁₆–¹/₈in) thick. Using the star cutter, cut out several star shapes. Repeat with the yellow fondant, and allow the starfish to dry for 1 day.

Keep the top and side edges crisp and sharp.

Swirl the buttercream using a palette knife for a watery effect.

5 Place the cake on a sheet of greaseproof paper. Put three-quarters of the buttercream icing into a separate bowl. Add 1 teaspoon of the aqua colouring paste and mix well. Cover the cake with the aqua buttercream using a palette knife. To smooth the edges, dip the palette knife in warm water and run it over the buttercream.

6 Add ¼ teaspoon of the brown colouring paste to the remaining untinted buttercream icing and mix well. Using a palette knife, paddle the brown icing around the bottom of the cake, so that it is textured and slightly rippled.

7 While the buttercream is still soft, press the gold glitter onto the brown icing to create the look of sand (you can also use soft light brown sugar for this). Put the cake aside to set for 2–3 hours.

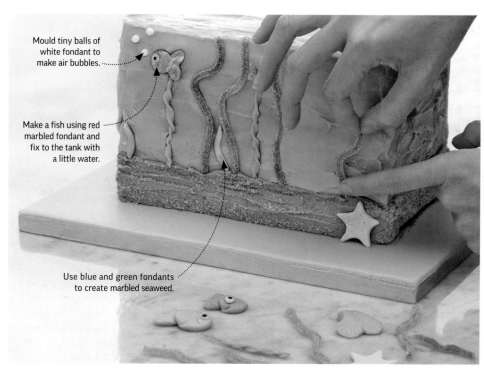

Mould tiny balls of white fondant to make air bubbles. ··········

Make a fish using red marbled fondant and fix to the tank with a little water.

Use blue and green fondants to create marbled seaweed.

8 Carefully move the cake to the covered cake drum. Fix all the sea elements to the cake using a little water. Cut the jelly laces and press into the buttercream in wavy patterns. Snip off any excess at the top. Press the goldfish tail onto the top of the cake. Finally, fix the blue ribbon in place around the base of the covered drum, using craft glue.

Under the Sea Cupcakes

Use a large round nozzle to pipe yellow buttercream onto the surface of the cupcakes, top with glitter, and then create sea creatures to decorate. A smiling starfish can be modelled using lilac fondant. Model a crab from deep pink fondant, creating eyes on stalks. For the coral, roll tiny balls of orange fondant and create a cavity with the end of a paintbrush. Score the surface of short ropes of green fondant for seaweed. All creatures need to harden for a few hours before you fix them to the cupcakes, using a little water.

Sea creatures

If you've got some spare time, why not try making some fishy cake pops (see p73) in a range of colours or use some leftover fondant to make some cheeky octopuses (see p72).

Press spaghetti sticks into a ball of white fondant and smooth down for the eyes.

Score a mouth with a circular cutter.

Use scissors to snip a small V-shape for the claws.

Try using yellow sugar crystals instead of glitter.

Score with the tip of a fine piping nozzle, or a star cutter.

Hand-modelling the lilac fondant gives a more realistic shape than using a cutter.

Blue paper cases complete the underwater theme.

Take one *cake pop...*

One cake pop – 12 different ideas to wow your party guests! Get creative and mould your cake pop into some weird and wonderful shapes then decorate with brightly coloured candy melts.

Pink fondant

Green fondant

Edible pen

Red candy melts

Apple

Moulded white fondant

Red sugar sprinkles

Blue candy melts

Brown candy melts

Edible pen

Band of white fondant

Piece of cake

Turquoise candy melts

Gold lustre dust

Ivory candy melts

Edible pen

Green fondant disc

Edible pen

Eyeball

Pink rice paper sprinkles

White fondant

Edible pen

Little star

Cover pop in white melts

Edible pen

sheet of white fondant

Ghost

Red candy-coated chocolate sweet

Rice paper sprinkles

Purple/pink candy melts

Brown candy melts

Ivory candy melts

Cupcakes

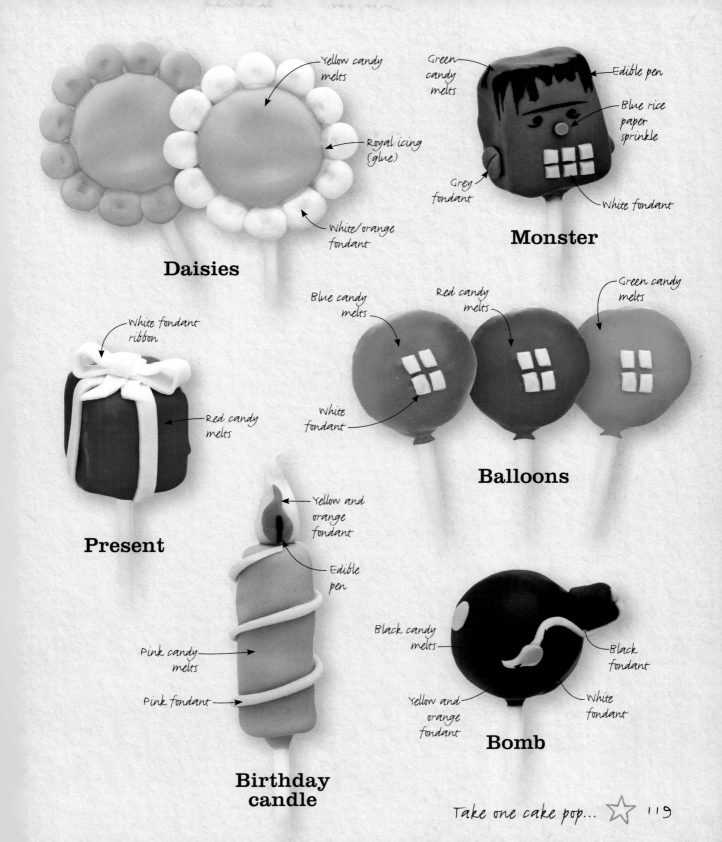

Daisies

Yellow candy melts

Royal icing (glue)

White/orange fondant

Monster

Green candy melts

Edible pen

Blue rice paper sprinkle

Grey fondant

White fondant

Present

White fondant ribbon

Red candy melts

Balloons

Blue candy melts

Red candy melts

Green candy melts

White fondant

Birthday candle

Yellow and orange fondant

Edible pen

Pink candy melts

Pink fondant

Bomb

Black candy melts

Black fondant

Yellow and orange fondant

White fondant

Take one cake pop... ☆ 119

Happy Robot

This cheerful robot is surprisingly easy to make, although care must be taken to support its large head with dowels and smaller cake boards. Spray with silver lustre, decorate with sweets of your choice, top with a cake-pop antenna, and prepare to delight a crowd.

PREP 1–1½ hrs   **BAKE** 1–1½ hrs   **DECORATE** 4 hrs, plus overnight drying time   **SERVES** 30–40

Ingredients

- icing sugar, for dusting
- 900g (2lb) pale-green fondant, strengthened (see p176)
- 4 x 20cm (8in) square cakes (see p186), layers sandwiched with buttercream to reach 20cm (8in) high and crumb coated (see p171)
- 3 x 15cm (6in) square cakes (see p186), layers sandwiched with buttercream to reach 15cm (6in) high and crumb coated (see p171)
- 4kg (9lb) pale-grey fondant
- 3 x 100ml can silver lustre spray
- 50g (1¾oz) royal icing (see p181)
- 400g (14oz) red fondant, strengthened
- 400g (14oz) bright-blue fondant, strengthened
- 50g (1¾oz) deep-yellow fondant, strengthened
- 25g (scant 1oz) each pale-blue, white, purple, and lemon-yellow fondant
- 25g (scant 1oz) black fondant
- black liquorice laces
- candy-coated chocolate buttons
- 1 cake pop, on stick, dipped in yellow candy melts (see pp172–3)

continued overleaf...

1 Dust a surface with icing sugar and roll out the strengthened green fondant to about 3mm (1/8in) thick, so that it is large enough to cover the surface of the larger cake drum. Moisten the surface of the drum. Cover the drum with the fondant, using the fondant smoother to create a smooth surface. Set aside to dry overnight.

2 Place the larger cake on the 20cm (8in) board. Dust a surface with icing sugar and roll out the some of the pale-grey fondant to about 5mm (1/4in) thick. Carefully cover the larger cake and board with the fondant and use the fondant smoother for an even surface. Trim off the excess fondant around the base using a sharp knife. Place the smaller cake on the 15cm (6in) board, roll out the grey fondant again, and cover as above. Ensure the excess is wrapped under the cake so that the bottom is almost covered. Allow to dry overnight.

Equipment

- fondant roller
- 40 x 35cm (16 x 14in) rectangular cake drum
- fondant smoother
- 20cm (8in) square cake board
- sharp knife
- 15cm (6in) square cake board
- 2 x 10cm (4in) square cake drums
- 4 plastic dowels, at least 20cm (8in) in height
- wire cutters or secateurs
- craft glue
- 2m (6½ft) red satin ribbon, 1cm (½in) wide
- blade tool
- 5 circular cutters – 6cm (2¼in), 7.5cm (3in), 5cm (2in), 4cm (1½in), 2cm (¾in)
- piping bag
- piping nozzle (PME no. 2)

3 When the fondant has set and become slightly harder and firmer to the touch, spray both the cakes with silver lustre spray, holding the can about 20cm (8in) away from the surface of the cake to provide an even finish. You may wish to spray the cakes on a newspaper-covered surface, as it can be messy. Allow to dry and then carefully move the cake to the covered cake drum.

4 Place one of the 10cm (4in) cake drums on the top of the larger cake and centre carefully. Gently press into the cake to emboss the surface, and then remove. Insert a dowel just inside the embossed mark and score it with a sharp knife at the point that it touches the top of the cake. Remove and cut the dowel at this mark using wire cutters. Cut the three remaining dowels to the same length.

5 Glue the two 10cm (4in) drums together to give extra height and fix two lengths of red ribbon all around the edges, using craft glue.

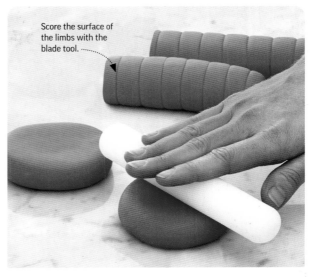

Score the surface of the limbs with the blade tool.

6 Insert a dowel into each of the four corners of the embossed square. Dab a little royal icing on the dowels and carefully place the covered drum on the cake taking care to fit it neatly over the embossed square.

7 For the arms and legs, roll two sausages each of the red and blue fondants. Roll and flatten two large balls of red fondant for the feet. Roll out some of the red fondant thinly, and cut a rectangle, 5 x 12cm (2 x 5in), for the front panel.

For the hands, cut out half-moon-shapes from the deep-yellow circles.

8 Roll two golf-ball-sized balls of bright blue fondant for the upper arms and flatten slightly. Roll out the deep-yellow fondant to 2cm (³/₄in) thick and cut out two circles with the 5.5cm (2in) circular cutter for the hands.

9 Roll out the pale-blue fondant to 5mm (¹/₄in) thick, and cut three circles using the 4cm (1¹/₂in) cutter, two using the 5cm (2in) cutter, and two using the 2cm (³/₄in) cutter. Then, roll out the white fondant to 5mm (¹/₄in) thick, and cut out two circles, using the 6cm (2¹/₄in) circular cutter.

Roll all the fondant
thinly on a dusted surface.

Layer one red and one
blue circle on the head
to hold the antenna later.

10 Cut out one 4cm (1¼in) circle from the purple fondant. Next, cut one 2cm (¾in) circle out of the lemon-yellow fondant and two from the black. Cut one 5cm (2in) circle and two 7.5cm (3in) circles from the remaining red fondant.

11 Layer the white, blue, and black circles on the smaller cake, using a little water, to create the eyes. Place one red and two blue circles on each side of the head for the ears. Fix them in place using a little water.

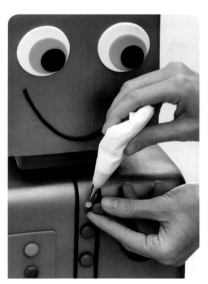

12 Fix the red rectangle to the front of the body with water. Fix the purple and lemon-yellow circles next to the rectangle with water.

13 Use liquorice laces for the front of the body and the mouth, fixing them in place using a little royal icing.

14 Fix the head on the top of the body using royal icing. Use more royal icing to glue rows of sweets on the front of the body and the ears.

Stick the cake pop on the top of the head.

Nuts and Bolts Cupcakes

These bright "robotic" cupcakes (see pp174–5) are great for feeding extra guests or filling party bags. Use a palette knife to ice cupcakes with buttercream coloured with different colouring pastes. Use plenty of paste to get a nice rich colour.

For the spring cupcake, roll a thin rope of strengthened fondant and then wrap it in spirals around a pen and leave to dry overnight. When dry, slip off the pen and cut into pieces. For the nut cupcake, cut out strengthened fondant circles using a cutter, and then cut a circle from the centre of each. Use the tip of a large circular piping nozzle to cut out semicircles from the perimeter.

For the bolt cupcake, roll a thicker rope of strengthened fondant and score the surface with a knife to create the threads. Cut into lengths. Use a hexagon cutter to cut small tops for the bolts and fix to the scored ropes with water. Allow to dry until just hard, and spray with silver lustre, one side at a time.

15 To assemble the robot, fix the arms and legs to the body using royal icing or water. Top the arms with the blue balls, and fix the red feet to the legs. Fix the ribbon around the base, using craft glue. Just before displaying, place the orange hands in place at the base of the arms.

 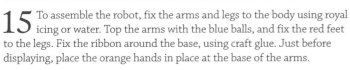

Sparkly Butterfly

Simply carve this beautiful butterfly out of a sheet cake, and decorate each wing before displaying around a buttercream-iced body coated in sugar strands. Experiment with a range of colours and sweets to bring your butterfly cake to life.

 PREP 40 mins   **BAKE** 30–45 mins   **DECORATE** 3–4 hrs, plus overnight drying time   **SERVES** 20

Ingredients

- cornflour, for dusting
- 500g (1lb 2oz) pale-green fondant, strenghtened (see p176)
- 30cm (12in) sheet cake, 7.5cm (3in) thick (see p164 and p186)
- 300g (10oz) buttercream icing, tinted pink (see p180)
- 200g (7oz) buttercream icing, tinted yellow
- 200g (7oz) buttercream icing, tinted purple
- 200g (7oz) buttercream icing, tinted turquoise
- 50g (1¾oz) edible yellow glitter
- 50g (1¾oz) edible purple glitter
- 250g (9oz) white fondant, strengthened
- 100g (3½oz) multi-coloured sugar strands
- assorted sweets – jelly beans, white chocolate discs topped with hundreds and thousands, hundreds and thousands, liquorice sweets, candy-coated chocolate buttons, red liquorice laces
- edible gold spray (or paint)
- 25g (scant 1oz) silver balls

continued overleaf...

1 Dust a surface with cornflour and roll out the pale-green fondant to about 3mm (⅛in) thick. It should be large enough to cover the cake drum. Use a pastry brush to moisten the drum with a little water and cover the drum with the fondant, then carefully smooth the fondant (see p179). Cut off any excess with a sharp knife and allow to dry overnight.

2 Place the sheet cake in the freezer for about 1 hour, until just beginning to freeze. Trace the template (see p187) onto a sheet of greaseproof paper, and cut out the individual elements. Press them down onto the surface of the slightly frozen cake, and cut around each with a serrated knife. Crumb coat each of the elements (see p171) with a little buttercream icing and refrigerate for 30–60 minutes, or until set.

Equipment

- fondant roller
- 30cm (12in) square cake drum
- pastry brush
- fondant smoother
- serrated knife
- palette knife
- side scraper (optional)
- 1 cake-pop stick, cut in half
- 1m (3¼ft) pink satin ribbon, 1cm (½in) wide
- craft glue

3 Set the cakes for the two top parts of the wings on a large piece of greaseproof paper. Using the palette knife, apply the pink buttercream. Reserve the remaining icing for later use. You can also use a side scraper, to achieve a smooth surface.

4 Repeat for the other parts of the wings, icing two in yellow buttercream, two in purple buttercream, and two in turquoise buttercream. While still soft, press the yellow glitter onto the top of the yellow wings and purple glitter onto the purple wings. Refrigerate all of the wings for 30 minutes.

5 Cover the body section of the butterfly with the remaining pink buttercream, then move to a plate and cover in multi-coloured sugar strands. Refrigerate for 30 minutes.

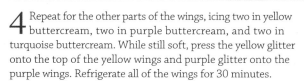

Use a palette knife to carefully place each wing on the drum.

6 To assemble the cake, arrange the body and wings as shown. Place the pink wings first, one on either side of the body, pressing them close to the body, followed by the yellow, purple, and turquoise wings.

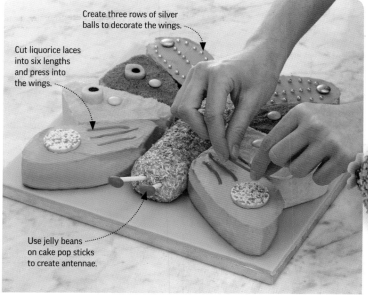

Create three rows of silver balls to decorate the wings.

Cut liquorice laces into six lengths and press into the wings.

Use jelly beans on cake pop sticks to create antennae.

7 Spray, or paint, two chocolate buttons gold, allow to dry, and place on the turquoise wings along with silver balls. Press yellow liquorice sweets and candy-coated chocolate buttons on the yellow parts. Repeat with the pink liquorice sweets and pink buttons on the purple parts. Place a white chocolate disc on the pink buttercream and decorate with liquorice. Finally, fix the ribbon around the base of the drum, using craft glue.

Flower Power Cake Pops

Complete the theme with pretty flower cake pops. Dip cake pops in melted chocolate or brown candy melts (see p173) and, before the coating hardens, dip half of the pops into a bowl of green-tinted sugar to cover about two-thirds of each pop. Roll out some pink fondant to about 2mm (¹⁄₁₆in) thick and use a blossom plunger cutter to create tiny flowers and a daisy plunger cutter in two sizes to create layers for the larger flowers.

Form centres for the larger flowers with tiny balls of yellow fondant, scored with a cocktail stick to provide texture. Fix the layers and the centre together with a little water and apply blossom and larger flowers to the cake pops with water or royal icing.

Green-tinted sugar strands or desiccated coconut is used to cover.

Melted chocolate or brown candy melts cover the cake pops.

sparkly Butterfly 129

Circus Big Top

This show-stopper cake is created from three sandwiched sponge cakes and an inverted bowl cake, and covered with brightly coloured fondant detail. The curtains are pulled back to reveal hand-modelled circus animals and a clown.

 PREP 1½ hrs

 BAKE 50-60 mins

 DECORATE 4½-5 hrs, plus overnight drying time

 SERVES 30

Ingredients

- cornflour, for dusting
- 300g (10oz) green fondant, strengthened (see p176)
- 3 x 20cm (8in) round sponge cakes (see p164), halved and sandwiched with buttercream (see p171)
- 20cm (8in) bowl or hemisphere cake (see p164)
- 500g (1lb 2oz) buttercream icing(see p180)
- icing sugar, for dusting
- 500g (1lb 2oz) white fondant (see p176)
- 500g (1lb 2oz) red fondant
- 300g (10oz) black fondant
- 500g (1lb 2oz) blue fondant
- 25g (scant 1oz) royal icing
- 500g (1lb 2oz) yellow fondant
- edible black pen
- 200g (7oz) ochre fondant, strengthened (see p176)
- 100g (3½oz) dark brown fondant
- 50g (1¾oz) orange fondant, strengthened
- 100g (3½oz) grey fondant, strengthened
- 20g (¾oz) light brown fondant, strengthened
- 25g (scant 1oz) white chocolate
- popcorn, for decorating

continued overleaf...

1 Dust a surface with cornflour and roll out the green fondant to about 3mm (⅛in) thick, so that it is large enough to cover the cake drum. Brush the cake drum with a little water and cover with the fondant. Use the smoother to create an even surface and cut off any excess using a sharp knife. Set aside to dry overnight. Wrap the remaining green fondant in cling film for later use.

2 Place a sandwiched sponge cake on a sheet of greaseproof paper, and paddle some buttercream on top using the palette knife. Carefully centre the second sponge cake on top of this and apply some more buttercream over it. Repeat with the final cake and then place the inverted bowl cake on top of this. Crumb coat the entire surface of the cake with buttercream (see p171) and refrigerate for 1 hour, until set.

Equipment

- fondant roller
- 30cm (12in) cake drum
- fondant smoother
- sharp knife
- palette knife
- 1 plastic dowel
- 23cm (9in) cake board,
- Dresden tool
- quilting tool
- ruler
- 2 circular cutters – 5cm (2in) and 2.5cm (1in)
- 3 cake-pop sticks
- small star-shaped plunger cutter
- large spatula or cake lifter
- ball tool
- paintbrush
- 24-gauge white floral wire
- piping bag
- piping nozzle (PME no. 1.5)
- 1m (3¼ft) blue satin ribbon, 1cm (½in) wide
- craft glue

3 Once the cake has set, insert the dowel through the centre of the cake, cutting off any extra that protrudes from the top. Apply a second coat of buttercream to the cake before beginning the decorations.

4 To make the roof, use the cake board as a template and draw a circle on a sheet of greaseproof paper. Cut around the circle, then fold it in half three times to get a neat wedge. Open the paper to get a circle marked with eight triangles.

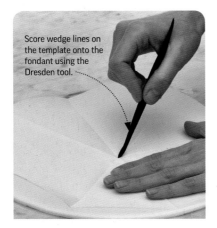

Score wedge lines on the template onto the fondant using the Dresden tool.

5 On a dusted surface, roll out the white fondant to 3mm (⅛in) thick to cover the roof template. With the template on top, cut a circle, then cut it into four wedges.

Use the quilting tool to score the surface of the wedges around the perimeter.

6 For the roof, moisten the backs of the wedges and place them opposite each other on the cake at even intervals. Cut off extra fondant to leave a cavity at the top. Trim off any excess.

Score the surface of the red wedges with the quilting tool.

7 Repeat steps 5 and 6 using the red fondant, to get four red wedges to fit between the white wedges on the roof. Trim to size and fix in place with water, ensuring their edges are flush, and score.

Use the fondant smoother to get an even surface.

8 Dust a surface with icing sugar and roll out most of the black fondant to 3mm (¹/₈in) thick. Use a ruler to measure the height from the base of the cake to the bottom edge of the roof. Using a sharp knife, cut out a rectangle from the fondant – as wide as the measured height, and about 17.5cm (6³/₄in) long. Moisten the back with a little water and press into position on the front of the cake. Trim off any excess.

9 Dust a surface with icing sugar and roll out the blue fondant to 3mm (¹/₈in) thick. Using a sharp knife, cut out a rectangle that is exactly as wide as the measured height, and long enough to wrap around the cake, just covering the edges of the black rectangle on the front. Moisten the back of the rectangle and smooth into place with your hands – use the fondant smoother to achieve an even finish.

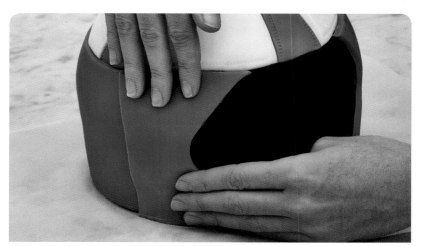

10 To make the curtains, roll out some of the remaining blue fondant again on the dusted surface to 3mm (¹/₈in) thick and cut out two rectangles that are exactly as tall as the height measured in step 8 and about 7.5cm (3in) wide. Cut out a curved triangle indent from one side of each curtain. Fix these into place on either side of the black fondant, using a little water, so that part of the curtain covers the black fondant and the remainder sits on the blue fondant wrapped around the cake.

11 To create a cap for the roof, re-roll the scraps of blue fondant on the dusted surface to 3mm (¹/₈in) thick. Cut out a circle using the larger circular cutter. Brush its back with water and gently press into place on the top of the roof.

12 Dust a surface with icing sugar and roll out the white fondant to 5mm (¼in) thick. Using the 2.5cm (1in) circular cutter, cut out about 30 circles. Roll a thin rope of the fondant to wrap around the base of the roof.

13 Cut all the white circles in half, and fix some around the blue cap on the roof with a little water. Fix the remaining semicircles around the base of the roof on the blue fondant. Fix the white rope in place with water around the top of the bunting.

14 Model a cherry-sized ball of white fondant, flatten, and fix to the top of the roof with water. Roll a smaller ball for the top of the flagpole, and leave to harden. Use a little more white fondant to model two cylindrical snack boxes. Set aside to dry.

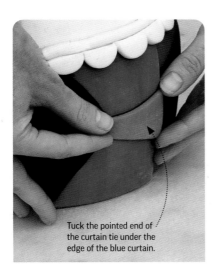

Tuck the pointed end of the curtain tie under the edge of the blue curtain.

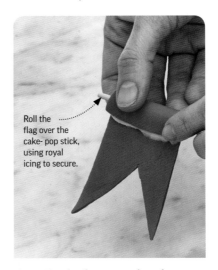

Roll the flag over the cake-pop stick, using royal icing to secure.

15 To make the curtain ties, dust a surface with icing sugar, roll out some of the red fondant to 3mm (⅛in) thick, and cut out two triangular wedges. Brush the backs with water and fix in place on the blue curtains.

16 To complete the popcorn snack box, roll a thin rope of the red fondant and flatten slightly. Cut the rope into tiny pieces to create stripes on the snack box.

17 For the flag, strengthen the remaining red fondant (see p176) and roll to 3mm (⅛in) thick. Cut out a rectangular piece and then cut a triangle from one end. Fix a cake-pop stick at the straight end and set aside to dry.

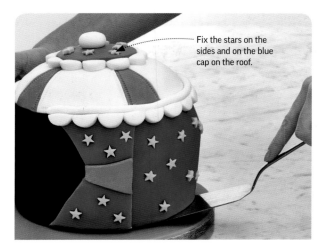

Fix the stars on the sides and on the blue cap on the roof.

Cut a cross in each eye with a knife, and trace with the edible black pen.

Moisten the base of the hat and fix to the head at a jaunty angle.

18 Dust a surface with icing sugar and roll out the yellow fondant to 3mm (¹⁄₈in) thick. Using the plunger cutter, cut stars to decorate the cake. Fix in place with a little water. Set aside to dry. When the cake is firm, use a large spatula or cake lifter to move it to the centre of the cake drum. Set aside to dry overnight.

19 For the clown, strengthen the remaining white fondant (see p176) and roll a golf-ball-sized ball. Roll two tiny balls for the eyes and flatten slightly. Score and fix on the face with water. For the hat, strengthen the black fondant and roll it out on a dusted surface to 3mm (¹⁄₈in) thick. Cut out a circle 2.5cm (1in) wide. Model a cylinder from the remaining fondant and fix on the circle using water. Fix the hat on the head.

Use the tip of the ball tool to create a cavity in the centre of the ears.

20 To finish the clown, roll about 20 tiny balls of varying sizes from the red fondant. Fix one ball to the face with a little water to create the nose, and the others around the hat for hair. Roll a small sausage for the mouth, and fix to the face. Score a smile using a knife. Set the clown aside to dry, ideally for 1–2 days.

21 For the lion, model the ochre fondant into a golf-ball-sized ball for the head. Roll a smaller ball for the muzzle, flatten slightly, and fix on the face using water. Model two tiny balls for the ears and fix on the head with water. Roll a tiny ball of strengthened dark brown fondant, shape into an oval, flatten, and fix on the muzzle with water for the nose.

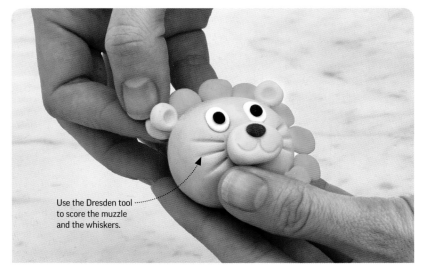

Use the Dresden tool to score the muzzle and the whiskers.

Use the Dresden tool to score wrinkles on the trunk.

22 For the eyes, roll two small balls of white fondant, flatten slightly with your fingers, and fix on the face using a little water. Roll two tiny balls of black fondant, flatten, and press into the white eyes. To make the mane, roll 12 pea-sized balls of the strengthened orange fondant, flatten slightly, and fix these around the head using a little water. Set aside to dry, ideally for 1–2 days.

23 For the elephant, roll the grey fondant into a golf-ball-sized ball for the head. Roll a rope of grey fondant for the trunk and cut each end to create a flat surface.

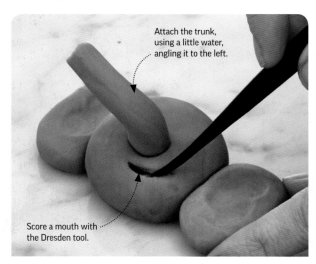

Attach the trunk, using a little water, angling it to the left.

Score a mouth with the Dresden tool.

Use the end of a paintbrush to create cavities in the centre of the white fondant.

24 Attach the trunk to the head using a little water, bending it slightly to the side. Roll two 2.5cm (1in) balls of the grey fondant and flatten into ovals, for the ears. Use the ball tool to create indentations in the ears, smoothing all the edges as you go. Moisten the sides and press the ears onto the head, and hold in place until firm.

25 For the eyes, roll two pea-sized balls of white fondant, flatten slightly, and fix to the face, just above the trunk, using a little water. Roll two tiny balls of the black fondant and press them into the centre of the white fondant eyes. Set the elephant aside to dry, ideally for 1–2 days.

Use the tip of the ball tool to create a cavity in the centre of each ear.

Mix together a little red and white fondant to create pink fondant for the nose.

Use the Dresden tool to score the muzzle.

26 To make the bear, roll a golf-ball-sized ball of the dark-brown fondant. Model a smaller ball for the muzzle, flatten slightly with your fingers, and fix on the face with water. Model two tiny balls for the ears. Moisten one side of each ear with water and press into place on the head.

27 For the eyes, roll two small balls of the white fondant, flatten slightly with your fingers, and fix on the face using a little water. Roll two tiny balls of the black fondant and press into the white eyes. Fix a tiny ball of strengthened pink fondant on the muzzle for the nose.

Score the bow with a knife to create folds.

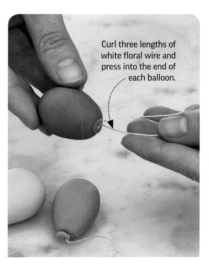

Curl three lengths of white floral wire and press into the end of each balloon.

Use the Dresden tool to score the surface of the peanuts.

28 Make two teardrop shapes out of the red fondant for the bow. Roll a pea-sized ball for the centre, and fix the bow together with water. Fix at the base of the head with water. Set aside to dry, ideally for 1–2 days.

29 Strengthen the remaining green, blue, and yellow fondants and model into balloon shapes. Fix a small flattened ball of fondant in each colour to the end of each balloon. Fix the floral wires and set aside to dry, for 1–2 days.

30 To complete the peanut snack box, roll a very thin rope of the blue fondant and flatten slightly. Cut the rope into tiny pieces to create stripes on the box. Create peanuts using the light brown fondant. Set aside to dry.

31 When everything is dry and hard, melt the white chocolate. Cut the cake-pop sticks in half and dip each end in the chocolate. Press one end of a cake-pop stick into the clown's head and the other end into the cake, holding the clown in place with your fingers until the chocolate hardens.

32 Fix all the animals with cake-pop sticks and chocolate, until they are firmly in place on the cake. Fix the balloons to the roof with white chocolate, holding in place until firm.

Pipe scallops on the front of the flag using royal icing. ....

Break the popcorn into little pieces and fix to the snack box with white chocolate.

33 Decorate the flag using royal icing and set aside to dry. Once dry, apply white chocolate to the end of the cake-pop stick and carefully push into the ball on the top of the roof. Use white chocolate to glue the smaller white fondant ball onto the top of the flagpole.

34 Fix the snack boxes on the cake drum using a little melted chocolate. Fix the popcorn on the red snack box and some peanuts on the top of the blue snack box using chocolate. Glue the remaining peanuts onto the cake drum with melted chocolate, so that they appear to tumble from the bags, and fix one at the end of the elephant's trunk.

35 Allow the decorations to set for 1 hour, then fix the blue ribbon around the base of the cake drum using craft glue.

Circus Party Cake Pops

Create gorgeous circus cake pops (see p172–3) for party take-homes or to accessorize your table. For the clown, dip the cake pop in melted white candy melts, allow to harden, and decorate as shown in steps 19–20.

For the popcorn box, mould the cake pop to shape, then dip in white candy melts. Once dry, draw on stripes with a red edible pen and fix a piece of popcorn to the top with white chocolate.

The bear cake pop is created by dipping a cake pop in melted brown candy melts or chocolate, and accessorizing with fondant ears, muzzle, eyes, and a length of blue ribbon at the base.

Cake *concepts*

If you're looking for a twist on a traditional cake, take a look at these cake concepts. Here you'll find inspiration for quirky centrepieces that the children can help to create, or demolish!

Jelly rainbow

Simply allow each thin layer of jelly to set in a mould before pouring on the next layer in another colour. Allow the jelly to cool a little before pouring.

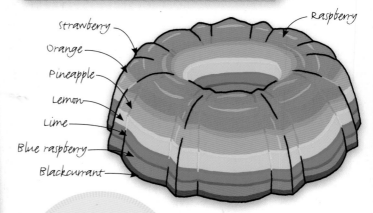

strawberry
Orange
Pineapple
Lemon
Lime
Blue raspberry
Blackcurrant
Raspberry

Doodle on it Ice a cake with white fondant, smooth the top and sides, and allow it to harden overnight. Supply edible pens in a variety of colours and let your child create a masterpiece!

Stack it up

Pile high a stack of delicious chocolate brownies and drizzle with melted white chocolate for the ultimate tower cake.

Ice cream sundae

Fill a cake tin with softened ice cream and broken biscuits, honeycomb, or sweets, then freeze until hard. Decorate with an upturned cone, a scoop of chocolate buttercream and melted chocolate.

Easy Dolly Varden

Ice a crumb-coated bowl cake with buttercream or fondant, then fix blossoms, leaves, and vines to the surface. Carefully carve a hole from the centre, and insert a plastic doll. Mould a bodice out of fondant, and attach dragées around the base and waist to draw it all together.

use blossom cutters to cut flowers out of fondant.

Piñata

Make a chocolate piñata by painting a thick layer of melted chocolate into a bowl lined with cling film. Chill until solid then turn out, remove the film, and fix sweets on the surface using melted chocolate. Overturn on a pile of candy treasures.

Print it Have your child's favourite character printed onto a rice paper sheet. Place on top of a cake iced with buttercream or fondant. Pipe some buttercream around the edge for an impressive finish.

Peekaboo
Cut out enough stars from pink and green sponge cakes (see p164) to run the length of your finished cake. Pour a little plain batter into a loaf tin, rest the row of stars along the length, packing them tightly so they don't move, then cover with the remaining batter and bake.

Cupcake Caterpillar

Simple, brightly coloured cupcakes are linked with a star of buttercream and decorated with a variety of shop-bought treats to create this jolly little caterpillar. You can add more cupcakes to feed extra guests, and with no cake to cut, the mess will be minimal.

 PREP 45 mins, plus cooling time   **BAKE** 15 mins   **DECORATE** 30–45 mins   **SERVES** 15

Ingredients

- 1½ batches of vanilla sponge batter, or enough to make 15 cupcakes (see p164)
- 1 tsp red colouring paste
- 1 tsp green colouring paste
- 1 tsp blue colouring paste
- 1 tsp yellow colouring paste
- 400g (14oz) vanilla buttercream icing (see p180)
- 2 white chocolate buttons
- 50g (1¾oz) royal icing (see p181)
- 2 blue and 1 red candy-coated chocolate drops
- 1 red liquorice lace
- 2 red jelly beans
- 14 frosted jelly snakes, halved

Equipment

- 15 plain paper cases
- 2 piping nozzles – fine tip (PME no. 2) and large open-star (PME Supatube no. 13)
- 2 piping bags – 1 large and 1 small
- palette knife
- 1 cake-pop stick, cut in half

1 Preheat the oven to 180°C (350°F/Gas 4). Divide the batter between four bowls, add 1 teaspoon of a single colour of the colouring paste to each bowl. Blend well to create red, blue, green, and yellow batters. Fill four cupcake cases with yellow batter, four with red, four with green, and three with blue. Bake for 15 minutes, or until the cupcakes have risen nicely and spring back to the touch. Allow to cool for 1 hour on a wire rack.

2 Remove the cooled cupcakes from the wire rack. On a tray or board, arrange the cupcakes on their sides in an inverted S-shape. Place the red cupcake first, followed by the green, yellow, and blue ones. End the caterpillar with the last red cupcake, reserving a green and a yellow cupcake for the head.

3 Fit the star nozzle onto the large piping bag and fill with buttercream icing. Pipe some of the icing onto the centre of each of the cupcakes.

4 Fit the cupcakes together, in the sequence laid out in step 2, leaving the green and yellow cupcakes aside for the head of the caterpillar.

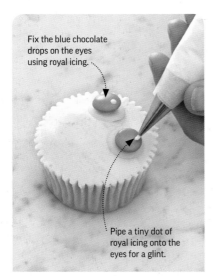

Fix the blue chocolate drops on the eyes using royal icing.

Pipe a tiny dot of royal icing onto the eyes for a glint.

5 For the face, smooth buttercream over the reserved yellow cupcake using a palette knife. Press two white-chocolate buttons onto the cupcake for the base of the eyes.

6 Use a red candy-covered chocolate drop for the nose and a liquorice lace for the mouth. Position the head onto the green cupcake, fixing it in place on some piped buttercream icing.

7 Top each half of the cake-pop stick with a jelly bean and carefully poke into the caterpillar's head to form the antennae.

8 To create the legs of the caterpillar, use buttercream or royal icing to fix the jelly snakes to the sides of the cupcakes making up the body. Allow to set for 30 minutes before serving.

Caterpillar Cupcakes

Create these simple caterpillar faces to serve with the cake or to send out in party bags. Use plain or tinted sponge for the base (see p164), or add a little colour by using cupcake cases in any number of colours. Simply spread with buttercream, using a palette knife, and then top with white chocolate buttons and brightly coloured candy-covered chocolate drops for the eyes (with a piped dot of royal icing to create a glint). Decorate with liquorice laces and more sweets, if desired. Jelly beans on cake-pop sticks make perfect antennae.

Princess Castle

Fit for a princess, this elegant cake is created from tiered sponge cakes, iced with silky buttercream, and surrounded by stacked cookie towers that have been iced and then topped with waffle cones. A pretty princess looks down from the balcony onto a lawn full of roses.

 PREP 1½hrs   **BAKE** 50-60 mins   **DECORATE** 4½-5 hrs, plus overnight drying time   **SERVES** 30-40

Ingredients

- 200g (7oz) buttercream icing, tinted pale green (see p180)
- 2 x 20cm (8in) round sponge cakes (see p164), sandwiched with buttercream and crumb coated (see p171)
- 2 x 13cm (5½in) round sponge cakes, sandwiched with buttercream and crumb coated
- 1kg (2¼lb) ivory buttercream
- 200g (7oz) white chocolate
- 4 x 250g packet chocolate chip cookies
- 50g (1¾oz) flesh-coloured fondant, strengthened (see p176)
- 50g (1¾oz) rose-coloured fondant, strengthened
- dry spaghetti
- 25g (scant 1oz) reddish-brown fondant, strengthened
- edible black pen
- 50g (1¾oz) small sugar pearls
- edible pink lustre dust
- 50g (1¾oz) fuchsia fondant
- cornflour, for dusting
- 200g (7oz) pale-pink fondant
- 50g (1¾oz) pale-green fondant
- icing sugar, for dusting
- 2 small silver sugar balls
- 4 waffle cones
- 3 tbsp royal icing (see p181)

continued overleaf...

1 Spread some of the pale-green buttercream icing over the cake drum using the palette knife. To achieve an even surface, dip the knife in warm water, dry, and then smooth over the icing. Allow the cake drum to set overnight.

Dip the knife in warm water, dry, and smooth over the icing to get an even surface.

Snip the dowels so that they are flush with the cake surface.

2 Place the 20cm (8in) sandwiched cakes on greaseproof paper. Apply the ivory buttercream all over using the palette knife. Repeat with the smaller cakes. Leave to set overnight.

3 Move the larger cake onto the iced drum. Gently press the 13cm (5½in) board into the top, centring it carefully, so that it leaves an imprint. Remove, then insert the dowels into the cake.

- 50g (1¾oz) hundreds and thousands
- 50g (1¾oz) white chocolate disc sweets covered with hundreds and thousands
- a little milk (optional)
- 100g (3½oz) white chocolate buttons
- sugar pearls
- 200g (7oz) white and pink miniature marshmallows
- 1 tsp white fondant

Equipment

- 35cm (14in) cake drum
- palette knife
- 13cm (5½in) cake board
- 4 plastic dowels
- small scissors
- small circle-tipped piping nozzle (PME no. 1)
- small artist's paintbrush
- fondant roller
- sharp knife
- cocktail stick
- shield cutters – 8cm (3¼in) and 4cm (1½in) (see p187 for templates)
- heart-shaped cutters – 4cm (1½in) and 1cm (½in)
- 1 cake-pop stick
- serrated knife
- piping bag
- 10cm (4in) thin pink satin ribbon
- 1m (3¼ft) pink satin ribbon, 1cm (½in) wide
- craft glue

4 Place the smaller cake on the 13cm (5½in) cake board, holding it in place with buttercream, then carefully place it on top of the larger cake using a palette knife. Apply some buttercream to hold the cake board in place. Leave to set overnight.

Buttercream heavily to fill in gaps between the biscuits.

5 Melt half the white chocolate, and use it to sandwich the chocolate chip cookies into four towers – use 19 cookies for every tower. Allow the towers to harden for about 30 minutes.

6 Use the palette knife to crumb coat with a layer of ivory buttercream, filling all the gaps. Chill the towers in the fridge, and then cover with another layer of buttercream. Leave to set overnight.

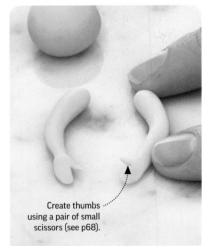

Create thumbs
using a pair of small
scissors (see p68).

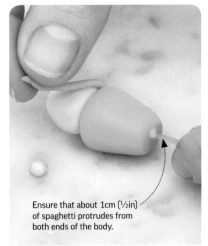

Ensure that about 1cm (½in)
of spaghetti protrudes from
both ends of the body.

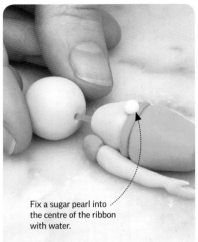

Fix a sugar pearl into
the centre of the ribbon
with water.

7 To make the princess, roll the flesh fondant into a large gumball-sized ball and model into a gentle oval to form the head. Use more fondant to model a slim neck and décolletage, and two arms, gently curved at the elbow.

8 Model a tapered torso from the rose-coloured fondant and attach to the décolletage using dry spaghetti. Make a thin rope of the rose fondant and wrap around the top of the torso to hide the join, fixing in place with water.

9 Create two cap sleeves from pea-sized balls of rose fondant and fix to the top of the arms with water. Fix the arms at the shoulders using a little water. Moisten the base of the head and slip onto the spaghetti.

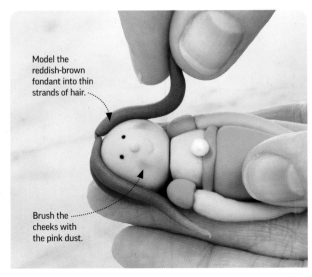

Model the
reddish-brown
fondant into thin
strands of hair.

Brush the
cheeks with
the pink dust.

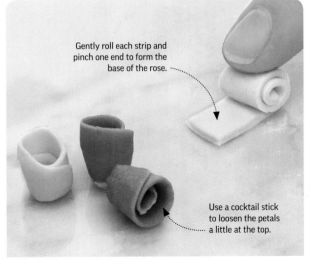

Gently roll each strip and
pinch one end to form the
base of the rose.

Use a cocktail stick
to loosen the petals
a little at the top.

10 Create a nose with a tiny ball of the flesh fondant, and dot two eyes with the edible black pen. Use the end of a piping nozzle to score a smile. Fix the hair into place with water, giving it a side parting. Set three sugar pearls into the hair to create a tiara. Leave to set overnight.

11 Dust a surface with cornflour and roll out some of the pale pink fondant very thinly. Carefully cut out ribbons, about 5mm (¼in) wide. Cut these to 2.5cm (1in) long pieces and roll to make about 20 small roses. Repeat with the fuchsia fondant to create 20 more roses. Set aside.

12 To make the vines, roll some of the pale-green fondant to form thin ropes. From the remaining fondant, model about 30 small teardrop-shaped leaves. Score the veins using a sharp knife. Set aside to dry.

13 Once the cookie towers have set, place them on the cake drum around the cake tiers. Fix them in place using buttercream icing, or melted white chocolate, spread on the base of each tower.

14 For the windows, dust a surface with icing sugar and roll out most of the remaining pink fondant to 2–3mm (1/16–1/8in) thick. Use the small shield cutter to make 17 windows, and create the panes with a knife.

15 Moisten the backs of the windows with a little water, and press into place on the cakes and towers. Fix three windows on the back and front of the top tier, and attach three windows on the back of the lower tier.

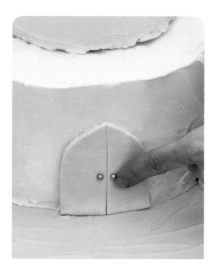

16 With the large shield cutter, create a door from the rolled-out pink fondant and score a line down the centre. Fix to the cake with water and press two silver balls onto the surface with royal icing for doorknobs.

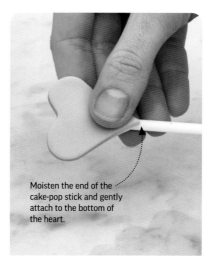

Moisten the end of the cake-pop stick and gently attach to the bottom of the heart.

17 Dust a surface with cornflour and roll the remaining pink fondant to about 3mm (1/8in) thick. Use the large heart-shaped cutter to cut out a pink heart. Attach to the cake-pop stick and set aside to dry.

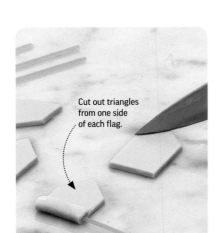

Cut out triangles
from one side
of each flag.

18 Cut out four flags from the rolled-out pink fondant, using a sharp knife, and attach onto four small pieces of spaghetti. Set the flags aside to dry.

19 To make the tower tops, use the serrated knife to trim the base of the waffle cones, so that they are as even as possible. Melt the remaining white chocolate, dip the tips of the cones, one by one, into the white chocolate, and immediately roll in a small bowl of hundreds and thousands. Allow to harden, and then use white chocolate to fix the cones on top of the towers.

20 To decorate the towers, halve the white chocolate discs covered in hundreds and thousands and fix around the base of the cones with a little melted white chocolate. Fix another row of white chocolate buttons below the cones, using a little more melted chocolate.

21 To finish the towers, roll four small balls out of the remaining pale-green fondant and flatten at the base. Moisten the bases with a little water and press onto the tops of the cone roofs. Carefully press the flagpoles into the green tops.

22 Soften the remaining green buttercream with a little milk, or heat in the microwave, to piping consistency. Fill a piping bag with the buttercream and dot the backs of five white chocolate buttons, one at a time. Press the buttons in front of the door to get a neat row. Repeat to get four rows.

23 Using a little royal icing, or buttercream, fix the sugar pearls around the base of both the cake tiers and the four towers to form a border around the entire castle.

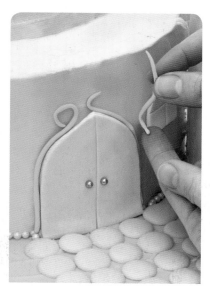

24 Brush the backs of the green vines with a little water, and press into place around the door in a decorative pattern.

25 Pipe a dot of buttercream at the base of each rose and fix along the sides of the path, at the base of the front towers, on the surface of the lower tier, and around the cake drum. Fix 1–2 green leaves around some of the roses.

26 Apply buttercream onto the base of the marshmallows and stick into place around the top perimeter of each cake tier, alternating pink and white marshmallows. Fix the princess in place with a little water.

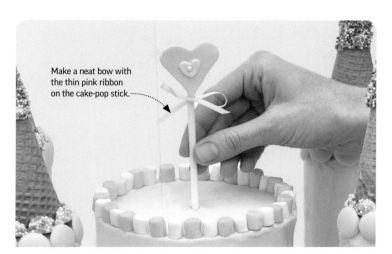

Make a neat bow with the thin pink ribbon on the cake-pop stick.

27 Dust a surface with cornflour and roll out the white fondant very thinly. Cut out a heart, using the small heart-shaped cutter. Fix a sugar pearl into the centre of the white heart using a little water. Fix the white heart to the centre of the larger pink heart and press the stick into the middle of the top of the castle.

28 Allow the cake to set for 1 hour. Use craft glue to fix the pink satin ribbon in place around the base of the drum.

Hearts and Flowers Cake Pops

Create a centrepiece with these delicate, exquisite cake pops (see pp172–3) and delight your little princess. To make the heart, mould the cake pop into shape with your fingers, before dipping into pink candy melts. Roll out a little ivory fondant very thinly and use a heart-shaped cutter to cut out a small heart. Fix in place on the pop with a little water and decorate.

For the rose, dip the cake pop in pink candy melts and allow to harden. Roll pink fondant very thinly and cut out nine petal shapes, using a petal cutter. Wrap the first petal around the pop, so that it is almost closed at the top. Moisten the base of another petal and fix to the first one. Repeat with the other petals, moving around the pop, so that three petals form the inside row, and five petals are placed around that. Roll out some green fondant, cut out a calyx with a star cutter, and fix below the rose with water.

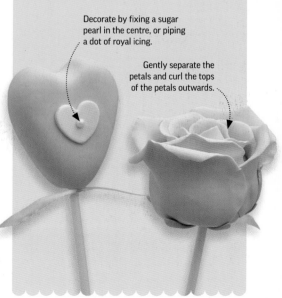

Decorate by fixing a sugar pearl in the centre, or piping a dot of royal icing.

Gently separate the petals and curl the tops of the petals outwards.

Flying Superhero

It's surprisingly easy to make this colourful cake, with simple buildings cut from flower paste and piped with yellow royal icing, and fondant lightning bolts, stars and explosions fixed onto bright blue icing. Decorate your superhero with coloured fondant to create your child's favourite character.

 PREP 1hr 20 mins   **BAKE** 25-30 mins   **DECORATE** 4-5 hrs, plus overnight drying time   **SERVES** 20

Ingredients

- cornflour, for dusting
- 100g (3½oz) blue-grey flower paste (see p177)
- 100g (3½oz) black flower paste
- 100g (3½oz) bright-blue flower paste
- 2 x 20cm (8in) round vanilla sponge cakes (see p164), sandwiched and crumb coated with buttercream (see p171)
- 200g (7oz) buttercream icing (see p180)
- icing sugar, for dusting
- 1kg (2¼lb) bright-blue fondant (see p176)
- 20g (¾oz) flesh-coloured fondant, strengthened
- dry spaghetti
- 20g (¾oz) black fondant, strengthened
- 200g (7oz) yellow fondant, strengthened
- 200g (7oz) red fondant, strengthened
- 50g (1¾oz) royal icing (see p181)
- 100g (3½oz) royal icing, tinted bright yellow

Equipment

- sharp knife
- palette knife

continued overleaf...

1 Dust a surface with cornflour and roll out the blue-grey, black, and bright-blue flower pastes to about 2mm (¹/₁₆in) thick. Use a sharp knife to cut rectangles for the buildings in different sizes and shapes (5–10cm/2–4in tall), altering the angle of the tops to create an interesting skyline. Leave to dry on a dusted plate for 2–3 days.

2 Refrigerate the sandwiched and crumb-coated cake to set for 30 minutes, then apply a second, light coat of buttercream icing with the palette knife (see p171). Dust a surface with icing sugar and roll out the bright-blue fondant to about 5mm (¼in) thick. It should be large enough to cover the top and sides of the cake. Use the fondant smoother to achieve a neat finish (see p178). Cut off the excess at the base and set aside to dry overnight.

- fondant roller
- fondant smoother
- modelling tool, or drinking straw
- edible black pen
- tweezers
- Dresden tool
- ball tool
- small sewing or nail scissors
- cocktail stick
- 10 cake-pop sticks
- 10cm x 8cm (4in x 3¼in) red fabric
- needle and red thread
- 1m (3¼ft) red satin ribbon, 3cm (1¼in) wide
- craft glue
- piping bag
- piping nozzles (PME no. 1, 2, and 3)

Use a drinking straw, cut in half, to emboss a smile on the superhero's face. ······

3 To make the superhero, roll the flesh-coloured fondant into a cherry-sized ball and mould into the shape of a head. Insert a small piece of dry spaghetti into the head for support. Use a modelling tool or a drinking straw to score a smile.

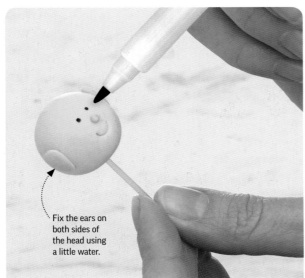

Fix the ears on both sides of the head using a little water.

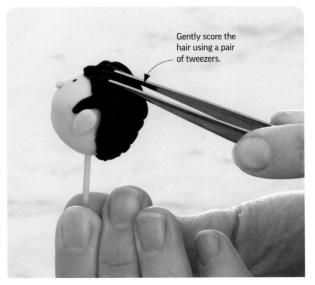

Gently score the hair using a pair of tweezers.

4 Draw two eyes using the edible black pen. Roll a pin-sized ball of the flesh-coloured fondant and place on the face for the nose. Roll two tiny balls of the fondant, flatten to form ears, and fix. Allow to dry overnight.

5 Roll a circle of fondant large enough to cover the back of the head. Shape the front to create a hairline and fix to the head using a little water. Create sideburns with extra strands. Allow to dry overnight.

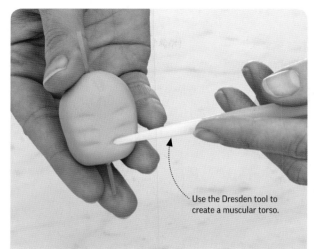

Use the Dresden tool to create a muscular torso.

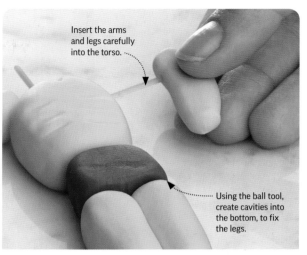

Insert the arms and legs carefully into the torso.

Using the ball tool, create cavities into the bottom, to fix the legs.

6 Form the torso by modelling the yellow fondant with your fingers to create the upper body, tapering it slightly towards the waist. Cut the bottom so that it will sit flush with the hip area. Insert a small piece of dry spaghetti right through the torso for support.

7 Roll a walnut-sized ball of the red fondant and flatten from all sides to create the shorts. Fix at the base of the torso. Roll two long sausages of yellow fondant for legs and taper towards the knee, to fit into the boots later. Roll two small sausages of yellow fondant for the upper arms, tapering towards the elbow. Hold everything in place with spaghetti.

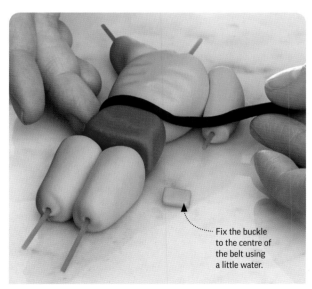

Fix the buckle to the centre of the belt using a little water.

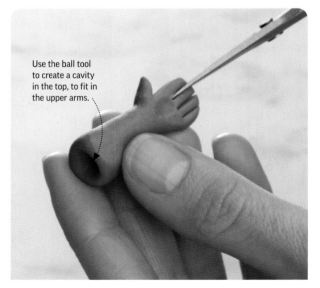

Use the ball tool to create a cavity in the top, to fit in the upper arms.

8 To make the belt, roll a thin rope of black fondant. Fix it around the superhero just above the red shorts. Make a tiny square of yellow fondant for the buckle and fix to the belt.

9 Model narrow cones of red fondant to create the gloves. Flatten one end and use small scissors to cut out the fingers. Use the cocktail stick as a mini rolling pin to soften the edges and define the shape. Set aside to harden slightly.

10 Model boots from two sausages of red fondant, cutting them off at the top and modelling the base to form the feet. Use the ball tool to create a cavity in the top into which the legs will fit. After a little drying time, moisten the tops of the boots with a little water and fix in place with the lengths of spaghetti. Carefully press a cake-pop stick into the top of the leg, to make a hole (see step 12 for positioning), and pull out the stick.

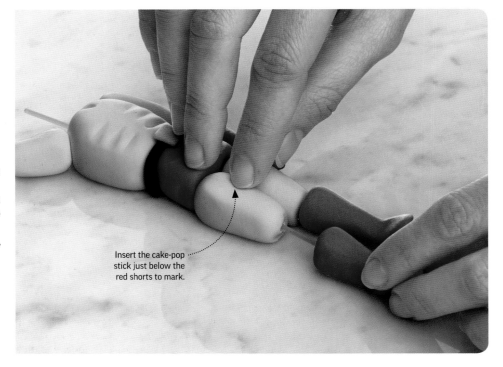

Insert the cake-pop stick just below the red shorts to mark.

11 Moisten the end of the red glove and fix to the spaghetti that is running through the arms. Once the head is dry, fix onto a pea-sized ball of strengthened yellow fondant, flattened, base moistened with water, and slipped onto the spaghetti at the top of the torso, to form a neck. Set aside to dry overnight.

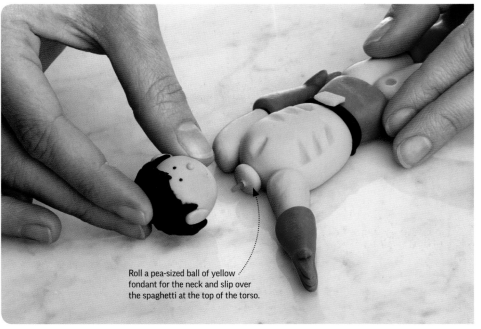

Roll a pea-sized ball of yellow fondant for the neck and slip over the spaghetti at the top of the torso.

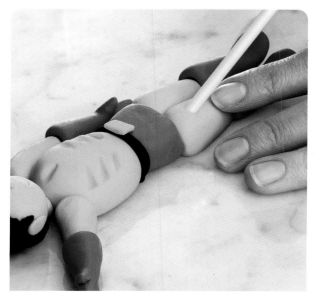

12 Apply a little royal icing to the end of a cake-pop stick and press it into the hole created in step 10.

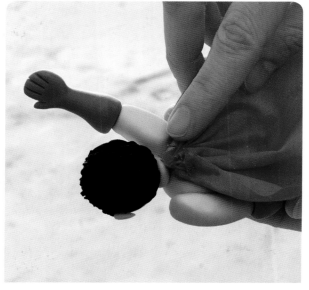

13 Cut out a square of red fabric, and carefully gather at the top, using a needle and thread to make running stitches. Pull the thread at one end so that the fabric bunches, and tie with a knot. Cut off the excess. Fix in place with royal icing.

14 When the cake has dried fully, roll out the remaining red, orange, and yellow fondant and use a sharp knife to cut out lightning bolts and stars in different sizes. Layer different colours of stars to create an explosion effect, fixing together with water. Allow to dry for 1 hour.

15 Move the cake to a presentation plate, if you wish. Fix the red satin ribbon around the base of the cake using a dot of royal icing. Fix the stars and bolts onto the cake in a random pattern using a little royal icing.

16 Fill the piping bag with yellow-tinted royal icing and use a variety of tips to pipe windows on the flower-paste buildings, using dots and lines. Use a little leftover yellow fondant, rolled very thinly, to create doors, if desired.

17 Press pieces of cake-pop sticks into the cake and fix the buildings to them by piping a line of royal icing up the back of each building. Press into place on the sticks to create an interesting skyline.

superpower Cupcakes

Create superpower treats, by spreading bright-yellow buttercream over the surface of baked, cooled cupcakes (see pp174–5). While they are setting, roll out yellow, orange, and red fondant to about 3mm ($^1/_8$in) thick, on a surface dusted with icing sugar. Use a sharp knife to cut star-like explosions in a variety of sizes. Allow to harden for 1–2 hours, and then layer the explosions, using a little water. Fix these to the surface of the cupcakes with a little buttercream.

If you have leftover fondant, try adding lightning bolts, or the crest of your child's favourite superhero.

Make your flying supergirl in the same way as the superhero in different colours, with long brown hair and a fluttering cape.

18 When the superhero figure is dry, press it into the top of the cake, so that it hovers over the skyline.

Take one *cupcake...*

You can transform a basic cupcake into one of these clever creations using shop-bought sweets and coloured fondant. Complete a theme or tailor-make a cake for each guest.

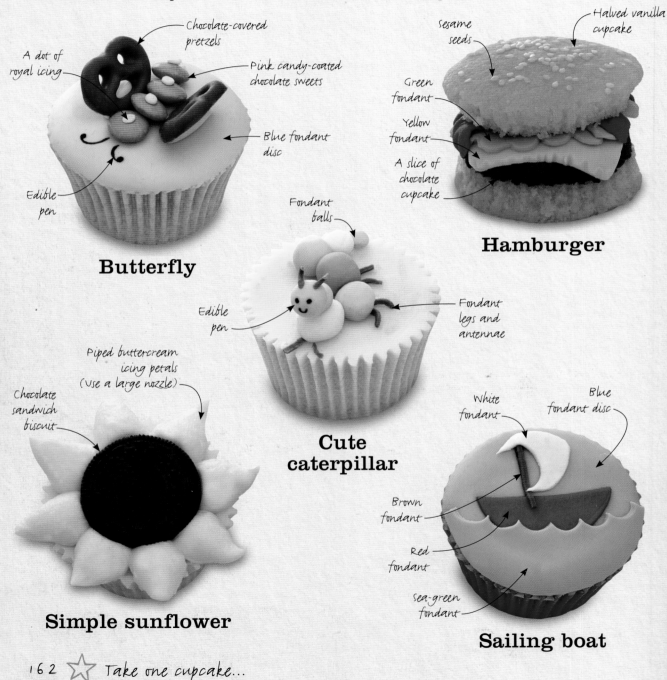

Chocolate-covered pretzels

A dot of royal icing

Pink candy-coated chocolate sweets

Blue fondant disc

Edible pen

Butterfly

sesame seeds

Halved vanilla cupcake

Green fondant

Yellow fondant

A slice of chocolate cupcake

Hamburger

Fondant balls

Edible pen

Fondant legs and antennae

Cute caterpillar

Piped buttercream icing petals (use a large nozzle)

Chocolate sandwich biscuit

Simple sunflower

White fondant

Blue fondant disc

Brown fondant

Red fondant

sea-green fondant

Sailing boat

Red fondant
disc

Red fondant

Black
fondant

White fondant
with edible pen

Ladybird

Crushed chocolate
biscuits

Chocolate
cupcake

Jelly
worms

Garden
worms

Yellow, black,
and white
fondant bee

Edible pen

Pale-brown
fondant over a
buttercream dome

Brown food
colouring mixed
with water and
brushed on

Dark brown
fondant

Chocolate
cupcake
crumbs

sea-green
fondant with
footprint shape
cut out

Prehistoric
print

Busy bee hive

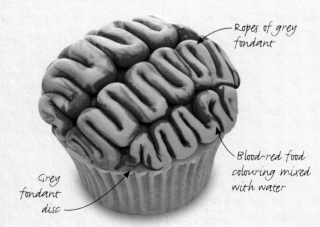

Ropes of grey
fondant

Blood-red food
colouring mixed
with water

Grey
fondant
disc

Brain power

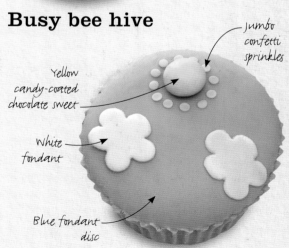

Jumbo
confetti
sprinkles

Yellow
candy-coated
chocolate sweet

White
fondant

Blue fondant
disc

Summer sky

Take one cupcake... 163

Sponge Cakes

A perfect cake not only looks great, but also tastes delicious. A classic sponge is an ideal base for most decorated cakes, and you can flavour it with a variety of natural extracts or ingredients to suit your taste. Denser cakes, like Madeira, are better for carving or heavy decorations.

Vanilla sponge

This sponge makes a good base for lots of different kinds of cakes, and can be adapted to incorporate many flavours. Use larger diameter tins for thin layers, and smaller tins for deeper ones.

PREP 20 mins   **BAKE** 25-30 mins   **SERVES** 10/makes 12 cupcakes

Ingredients

- 200g (7oz) unsalted butter
- 200g (7oz) caster sugar
- 4 eggs
- 1 tsp vanilla extract
- 200g (7oz) self-raising flour
- 1 tsp baking powder

Equipment

- electric whisk
- 2 x 20cm (8in) round cake tins, greased and lined (see p168)
- palette knife

Colouring sponges

Use colouring pastes or gels rather than liquids for vivid colours. Colours tend to deepen when baked, so add 1 teaspoon of paste or gel to the batter, blend, and check before adding more.

1 Preheat the oven to 180°C (350°F/ Gas 4). Soften the butter and whisk with the sugar in a bowl for 2 minutes, or until pale and fluffy.

3 Sift in the flour and baking powder, and gently fold in with a metal spoon, keeping the mixture light and smooth.

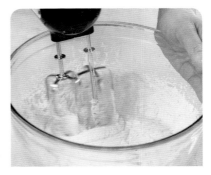

2 Add the eggs, one at a time, mixing well. Add the vanilla extract and whisk for 2 minutes, until bubbles appear on the surface.

To bake

Divide the mixture evenly between the tins, smoothing the surface with a palette knife. Bake for 25–30 minutes, or until a skewer comes out clean.

To finish

Cool the cakes in the tins for 10 minutes, and then turn onto a wire rack. When completely cool, fill as desired.

Madeira cake

Just a few simple ingredients are needed for this dense, buttery, lemon-flavoured cake. Replace lemon zest with 1¹/₂ teaspoon of vanilla extract, or any other flavour of your choice.

 PREP 20 mins   **BAKE** 50-60 mins   **SERVES** 10

Ingredients

- 200g (7oz) unsalted butter
- 200g (7oz) caster sugar
- 4 eggs
- 300g (10oz) self-raising flour
- grated zest of 1 lemon

Equipment

- 20cm (8in) round springform cake tin, greased and lined (see p168)

1 Preheat the oven to 180°C (350°F/Gas 4). Soften the butter and whisk with the sugar in a bowl until fluffy. Add the eggs, one at a time, mixing well as you go.

2 Whisk for 2 more minutes, until bubbles appear on the surface. Sift in the flour, add the zest, and gently fold in with a metal spoon until just smooth.

3 Spoon the batter into the tin, flatten using a palette knife, and bake for 50–60 minutes, or until a skewer comes out clean (see p169). Leave to cool in the tin for 10 minutes and then turn out onto a wire rack to cool completely.

Chocolate cake

An all-time favourite, the yogurt in this recipe makes this cake extra moist. It is delicious when filled with chocolate or vanilla buttercream.

 PREP 30 mins   **BAKE** 20-25 mins   **SERVES** 10/makes 12 cupcakes

Ingredients

- 200g (7oz) unsalted butter
- 200g (7oz) brown sugar
- 4 large eggs
- 150g (5¹/₂oz) self-raising flour
- 50g (1³/₄oz) cocoa powder
- 3 tsp baking powder
- 3 tbsp Greek yogurt

Equipment

- 2 x 20cm (8in) round cake tins, greased and lined (see p168)

1 Preheat the oven to 180°C (350°F/Gas 4). Soften the butter and whisk with the sugar in a bowl until light and fluffy. Add the eggs, one at a time, mixing well.

2 In a separate bowl, sift together all the dry ingredients. Fold the flour mixture into the butter and eggs batter with a metal spoon until well-blended. When the batter is light and fluffy, gently fold in the yogurt.

3 Divide the mixture evenly between the tins and bake for 20–25 minutes. Cool the cakes in the tins for 10 minutes, and then turn onto a wire rack. When completely cool, fill as desired.

Red velvet cake

This vivid red cake is traditionally topped with cream-cheese buttercream icing. Beetroot gives this cake its colour, but you can also use red colouring paste alongside the beetroot, if desired.

 PREP 50 mins   **BAKE** 35 mins   **SERVES** 10

Ingredients

- 3–4 medium beetroots, 500g (1lb 2oz) in total
- 300g (10oz) plain flour
- 50g (1¾oz) cocoa powder
- 2 tsp bicarbonate of soda
- ½ tsp salt
- 175g (6oz) unsalted butter, softened
- 275g (9½oz) brown sugar
- 200g (7oz) caster sugar
- 3 large eggs, at room temperature
- 2 tsp vanilla extract
- 100g (3½oz) dark chocolate, broken into pieces and melted
- 150ml (5fl oz) buttermilk mixed with 2 tsp cider vinegar
- cream-cheese buttercream icing (optional)

Equipment

- 2 x 20cm (8in) round cake tins, greased and lined (see p168)

1 Cook the beetroot in a pan half-filled with water for 30–40 minutes. Cool, then peel. Preheat the oven to 180°C (350°F/Gas 4).

3 In a separate bowl, whisk the butter, sugars, eggs, and vanilla extract, then add the cooled, melted chocolate. Whisk to form a uniform mixture.

2 Whizz the beetroot to a purée, adding a little water if needed. In a separate bowl, sift together the flour, cocoa, bicarbonate, and salt.

To bake

Slowly add the flour mixture and buttermilk–vinegar mix to the batter. Beat well. Stir in 250ml (9fl oz) of the beetroot purée, and mix well together. Divide the batter between the tins and bake for 35 minutes.

To finish

Cool and slice each cake in half horizontally. Layer the cake with cream cheese buttercream icing, if desired.

Carrot cake

This rich, moist cake is easy to make and works well in stacked and layered projects, as its density helps support weight. Cream-cheese buttercream icing makes for a perfect topping.

 PREP 20 mins   **BAKE** 45 mins   **SERVES** 10

Ingredients

- 100g (3½oz) walnuts
- 225ml (7½fl oz) sunflower oil
- 3 large eggs
- 225g (8oz) soft light brown sugar
- 1 tsp vanilla extract
- 200g (7oz) carrots, grated
- 100g (3½oz) sultanas
- 200g (7oz) self-raising flour, sifted
- 50g (1¾oz) wholemeal self-raising flour, sifted
- pinch of salt
- 1 tsp ground cinnamon
- 1 tsp ground ginger
- ¼ tsp grated nutmeg
- grated zest of 1 orange

Equipment

- 23cm (9in) round springform cake tin, greased and lined (see p168)

Walnuts add great flavour and texture to cakes.

1 Preheat the oven to 180°C (350°F/ Gas 4). Roast the walnuts for 5 minutes, rub with a tea towel, and roughly chop.

3 Squeeze the carrots dry and fold into the batter. Add the walnuts and sultanas, stir in the remaining ingredients, and mix.

2 Pour the oil and crack the eggs into a bowl. Add the sugar and vanilla extract, and whisk until smooth and thick in consistency.

To bake

Spread the batter into the tin, using a palette knife to smooth. Bake for 45 minutes, or until a skewer comes out clean (see p169).

To finish

Cool for 10 minutes in the tin, and then transfer to a wire rack to cool completely. If desired, slice horizontally and fill, or ice the top, with cream cheese buttercream icing.

Preparing a Cake

It is always worth taking your time to prepare your tins carefully to ensure even cooking of the cake and prevent them from sticking. Test with a skewer before removing from the oven, and always cool cakes on a rack before icing, filling, or decorating.

Preparing tins

Greasing Almost all cake tins, including non-stick tins, should be greased with butter, margarine, or oil. Use a pastry brush to ensure even coverage. Moulded tins, especially novelty tins, need greasing particularly well in the corners and crevices.

Lining Using baking parchment helps to prevent burning, particularly for cakes with longer cooking times. Make sure the parchment is smooth to avoid creating ridges in the cake.

1 Grease the tins well to ensure that the baking parchment sticks to the tin and does not move when the batter is poured.

2 Cut a strip of the baking parchment slightly longer than the circumference and slightly wider than the height of the tin. This ensures none of the batter goes through the parchment strips.

3 Fold the strip about 2.5cm (1in) from the long edge and make some evenly spaced cuts to the fold line using kitchen scissors.

4 Press the strip into the inside edge of the tin. Cut a circle from the baking parchment, using the bottom of the tin as a template, and fit in the base of the tin.

Dusting Sprinkle 1 tablespoon of plain flour into the bottom of the tin. Hold the tin over the sink, tilt it to move the flour from side to side, and tap the bottom to ensure even coverage. Discard the excess flour.

Baking and cooling

Make sure that cakes are cooked at the right temperature and for the correct length of time before you remove them from the oven. This ensures good consistency and optimum rising.

Baking Preheat the oven for 20 minutes before baking. Fan or convection ovens require a lower temperature than conventional ovens. If the recipe does not specify this, reduce the temperature by about 20°C (68°F). Pour the batter into the greased and lined tins and smooth the surface using a palette knife. Give the tin a few knocks against a hard surface before it goes into the oven, to release air bubbles. Don't open the oven – changes in temperature sometimes cause cakes to sink or to rise unevenly . If your oven heats unevenly, turn the cake after three-quarters of the cooking time. Cook for the entire time suggested by the recipe.

Testing There are two main ways to test a cake. The first is to press gently down in the centre of the cake with your finger. If it springs back, chances are it is ready. To be certain, insert a metal or wooden skewer into the centre of the cake. If it comes out clean, the cake is ready. Cakes in novelty tins can take longer to bake, so be sure to check the recommended time on the recipe provided on the tin packaging.

Cooling Cool a cake in its tin for about 10 minutes (a little longer if it is a deep, large cake), to help the cake keep its shape and "set". Then turn it out onto one wire rack and invert it onto another rack to cool completely. The base of your cake should be on the rack, not the top, to prevent it from losing its height and texture. Always make sure the cake is completely cool before icing and plating it, as this will prevent crumbling, breakage, and movement. If you are in a rush, you can chill your cake after it has been cooled in the tin.

Levelling

For a perfect finish, it is important to level your cake. Cool the cakes in the tin for 10 minutes before trimming the uneven bits. If your cake is lopsided or lumpy, cool completely before levelling.

Turntable method

Place the cake on a cake drum, and then on top of a turntable or lazy Susan. If it is not the drum you will be using for the finished cake, dust it first with icing sugar to ensure that the cake will not stick. Use a ruler and cocktail sticks pressed into the cake to mark your cutting line, to be sure it is even all the way round. Carefully turn the stand and gently move a serrated knife back and forth in a sawing motion to remove the dome, or any lumps, until you have a completely flat surface. Some people find it easier to freeze the cakes partially before levelling, which prevents chunks of cake being drawn up when you "saw" through it.

Cake leveller method

If you have a cake leveller, place the cake on a cake drum, over a firm surface, and carefully position the blade at the appropriate height. Gently saw into the side using a back and forth motion. Once you have got past the crust, simply glide the blade through the cake to the other side. If you are finding it tricky to keep the cake still while you cut, you can place it on a drum exactly the same size as the cake and pop the cake, on the drum, back into the cake tin. Level across the cake using the top edge of the tin.

Sandwiching

Sandwich thin layers of sponge cake to make it easier to carve. Ganache, whipped cream, jam, and fruit curds can also be used as fillings. Allow the filling to set before icing for best results.

Ingredients

- cooled cake layers, levelled
- buttercream icing (see p180)

Equipment

- cake drum
- turntable or lazy Susan
- piping bag with large, round tip
- palette knife

1 Move the base layer of the cake onto a drum and then onto a turntable. Fill the piping bag with icing and pipe around the inside edge. Place a spoonful of icing in the centre and spread with a palette knife.

2 Place the next layer on top, levelled side down. For two-layered cakes, you are now ready to crumb coat and ice. To build the cake higher, repeat, and finish with a levelled side down layer, for a level surface.

Crumb coating

Crumb coating is like adding a base coat to a wall before painting. It smoothes over any cracks or holes in the surface and helps the cake stay sealed and moist.

Ingredients

- 4 cakes, levelled, and layers filled with buttercream icing
- buttercream icing (see p180), thinned with a little milk

Equipment

- cake drum
- turntable or lazy Susan
- palette knife

1 Place the cake on a drum on a turntable. Use a palette knife to apply a thin layer of buttercream onto the cake. Start at the top of the cake and swirl the buttercream over the surface as you turn it around on the turntable.

2 Spread the icing around the sides until evenly covered. A few crumbs may be embedded in the icing, which is normal. Refrigerate, or allow to set for up to 2 hours. Apply the final layer of icing or fondant (see p178 and pp182–3).

Cake Pops

Cake pops are not only easy to make, but delicious too. Use them to accessorize cakes or to create treats for party bags. There are two main ways to make cake pops: the method below uses up leftover cake or use a tin, right, for purpose-made cake pops.

Using baked cake

Use whole cakes or leftover sponge to make perfect cake pops. This method works best for cake pops that are moulded into novelty shapes or simple balls. Leave to firm before dipping.

 PREP 10 mins, plus cooling

 MAKES 20-25

Ingredients

- 300g (10oz) sponge cake (see p164)
- 150g (5½oz) buttercream icing (see p180)

Insert cake-pop sticks into the balls and allow to set before dipping.

1 Blitz the whole cake, or leftover cake, in a food processor to create crumbs.

2 Place the cake crumbs in a bowl. Stir in the buttercream and mix until you get a smooth dough.

3 Using your hands, gently mould the cake mixture into uniform walnut-sized balls.

4 Place on a plate, with space between each, and refrigerate for 3 hours; or freeze them for 30 minutes.

Cake-pop tins

Use cake-pop tins to make uniform balls that are ready to dip and decorate. Dense sponges work better for making cake pops.

 PREP 20 mins   **BAKE** 15–18 mins   **MAKES** 12

Ingredients

- butter or oil, for greasing
- plain flour, for dusting
- ½ quantity Madeira cake batter (see p165)

Equipment

- 12-hole cake-pop tin
- skewer

1 Preheat the oven to 180°C (350°F/Gas 4). Grease and dust the tins. Spoon the batter into the bottom half of the tin (without holes) so that it mounds over the top of the tin. Cake-pop tins differ, so follow the instructions to ensure you use the correct amount of batter.

2 Place the top half of the tin on top and secure. Bake for 15–18 minutes. After baking time, test every 2 minutes with a skewer. Let the cakes cool in the tin for 10 minutes, and then turn out onto a wire rack to cool completely.

3 Chill the cake pops before decorating, so that they keep their shape.

Coating cake pops

Dip cake pops in candy melts or melted chocolate to provide a firm coating and the perfect canvas for decorating.

Ingredients

- melted chocolate
- 12 cake pops
- 200g (7oz) candy melts

Equipment

- 12 cake-pop sticks
- polystyrene

1 Dip one end of a cake-pop stick into a little melted chocolate and insert into the centre of a cake pop. Repeat with the remaining cake pops. Stand the cake pops upright in a piece of polystyrene, or an overturned colander, and chill for 20–30 minutes.

2 Melt the white candy melts. Dip cake pops into the melted candy, coating evenly. Allow excess to drip off.

3 Stand the cake pops upright in a piece of polystyrene, or an overturned colander, for 30 minutes, or until they harden.

Cupcakes

Cupcakes are ideal for parties, creating very little mess and requiring no plates. They can be iced with buttercream, topped with fondant, or simply filled and dusted with icing sugar. Make sure they are completely cool before decorating.

Preparing

Be sure not to overfill the cases, and cook for the correct length of time. Always preheat the oven for at least 20 minutes and prepare the tins before you begin to make the batter (see p164).

Using cases

Cupcake cases add a decorative element, make the cupcakes look neater, and help them remain fresh and moist for longer. If you choose to use a cupcake tin on its own, grease and dust it, brush with cake release products, or spray with a non-stick baking spray. Silicone cases do not require a cupcake tin. Fill and set them upright on a baking tray. Grease and dust them with plain flour to ensure that the cupcakes do not stick.

Filling

Fill the cupcake cases or tins about two-thirds full. Do not overfill as they can spill over the sides or develop a "nose". Standard-sized cupcakes require about 75ml (2^1/$_2$fl oz) of batter. For mini cupcakes, a heaped tablespoon of batter is enough. For special effects, layer different colours of batter into the cases with a piping bag. Create a surprise centre by popping sweets, or even a biscuit or a miniature brownie, into the centre before baking.

Baking

A standard-sized cupcake will take 18–20 minutes to bake, while mini cupcakes will take 8–10 minutes. They are ready if a skewer inserted in the middle of the cake comes out clean. When baking several tins at the same time, increase the baking time by a few minutes, and rotate the trays halfway through. Allow to cool in the tin for at least 10 minutes, and then cool on a wire rack. If you did not use cases, turn the cupcakes out onto your hand before placing them on the rack.

Piping

Cupcakes can be iced with a palette knife or, for a more professional finish, piped using one of a variety of different tips fitted onto a pastry or piping bag.

Ingredients
- medium-consistency buttercream icing (see p180)
- cooled cupcakes

Equipment
- piping bag with large open-star nozzle

1 Attach the nozzle to the piping bag and half-fill with the icing, so that the bag is easy to handle. Hold the tip 1cm (½in) above the cupcake, at a 90° angle, and pipe from the outside edge inwards, in a spiral.

2 Apply pressure evenly. Slowly increase the pressure at the centre, so that the icing forms a peak. Release the pressure to end the spiral at the centre of the cupcake.

Filling

Cupcakes can be filled with jam, buttercream icing, whipped cream, or even peanut butter, fruit mousses, and curds. Pop in a marshmallow or another treat before baking, for an extra surprise.

Cone method

With a sharp paring knife, cut out a cone shape from the centre of each cupcake. Slice off the tip of the cone and set aside. Spoon the filling of your choice into the cavity, stopping just before the top. Replace the lid and ice, as shown above.

Piping method

If you have thin, smooth icing or jam, you can use a plain round tip or a specialized injector tip on a piping bag. Attach the tip, load the piping bag with filling, and then insert it into the centre of the cupcake from the top. Gently press on the bag while piping, until the filling begins to expand out of the insertion hole. Ice and decorate as usual.

Fondant

This classic recipe works well both to cover cakes and to create decorations. Use food colouring paste to tint the fondant, bearing in mind that the colour deepens over time.

 PREP 20 mins **MAKES** 1kg (2¼lb)

Ingredients
- 2 sheets gelatine
- 120ml (4fl oz) liquid glucose
- 1 tbsp glycerine
- 1kg (2¼lb) icing sugar, plus extra for dusting
- colouring paste (optional)

Equipment
- cocktail stick

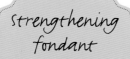

Strengthening fondant

For pliable fondant that hardens quickly without cracking, add 1 teaspoon tylose powder to every 200g (7oz) fondant.

1 Soak the gelatine sheets in cold water for 10 minutes. Wring dry and slowly dissolve in 60ml (2fl oz) warm water. Mix in the glucose and glycerine until well blended. Set aside.

2 Sift the sugar into a separate bowl. Create a well in the centre and pour in the liquid gelatine mix, a little at a time. Stir to form a soft ball.

3 Dust a surface with icing sugar and place the fondant onto it. Knead the fondant until it is smooth and pliable, adding a little water if it is too dry, or a little icing sugar if it is too tacky.

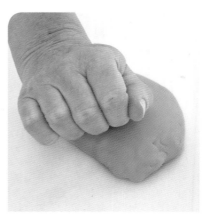

4 To colour the fondant, use a cocktail stick to apply a little colouring paste to the surface. Fold the fondant over the paste, and then knead until it has a uniform colour throughout.

Flower paste

Flower paste dries harder than fondant and can be rolled very thin for decorations, such as flowers. Although it is edible, it is not normally eaten. Colour it in the same way as the fondant.

 PREP 30 mins, plus thickening and chilling

 MAKES 500g (1lb 2oz)

Ingredients

- 2 tsp gelatine powder, dissolved in 5 tsp warm water and allowed to thicken for 30 minutes
- 2 tsp white vegetable fat
- 2 tsp liquid glucose
- 500g (1lb 2oz) icing sugar, sifted, plus extra for dusting
- 4 tsp tylose powder
- 1 egg white
- colouring paste (optional)

Equipment

- electric whisk

1 Place the thickened gelatine in a pan with the white vegetable fat and glucose. Stir over a low heat until the liquid is clear.

2 Transfer to the bowl and whisk in the icing sugar, tylose, and egg white. Turn the whisk up to the highest setting.

softening

Store flower paste in an airtight container. If the paste is sticky, add a little more white vegetable fat until smooth and pliable. If it is too hard and crumbly, add a little more beaten egg white.

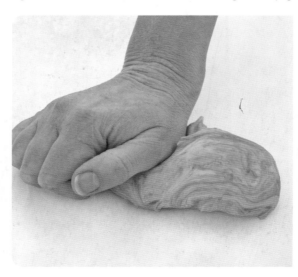

3 Continue to mix until stringy and white. Refrigerate the mixture for 1–2 days. Dust a surface with icing sugar and knead the mixture until it is smooth and pliable. Colour the paste in the same way as traditional fondant (see opposite).

Covering a cake

Covering with fondant provides a lovely canvas for decorations. Fondant can be applied over ganache, buttercream, or marzipan. The rolled fondant should be thick enough to avoid tearing.

Ingredients
- icing sugar, for dusting
- 1kg (2¼lb) fondant (see p176)
- 23cm (9in) 2-layer cake, crumb coated with buttercream (see p171)

Equipment
- fondant roller
- cake drum
- fondant smoother, plus one extra (optional)
- sharp knife

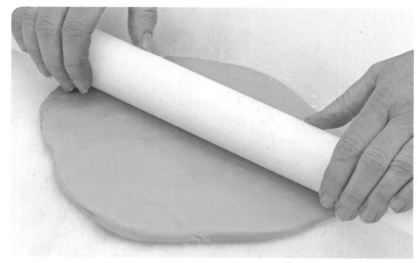

1 Dust a surface with icing sugar. Knead and roll the fondant into a circle that can cover the top and sides of the cake with, 5cm (2in) extra around the edges.

2 Cover the cake with the fondant sheet and smooth it across the top with a smoother, easing it down with your hands.

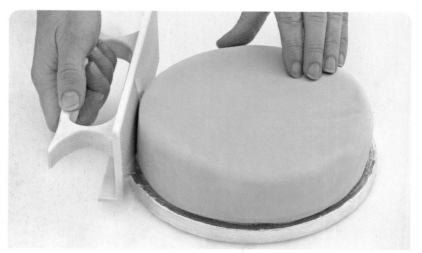

3 Trim off the excess fondant. Press the smoother evenly over the top of the cake, and then run it down and around the sides of the cake until perfectly smooth. To get a sharp edge at the top of the cake, you could use two smoothers at the same time, one on the top and the other on the sides, pressing them together at the edge.

  Covering a cake

Covering a cake drum

Cover cake drums in fondant, using various colours. You can emboss the fondant, add stripes or other detail, and even paint or dust it – set overnight before placing the cake on top.

Ingredients

- cornflour, for dusting
- 1kg (2¼lb) fondant, strengthened (see p176)
- tylose powder

Equipment

- fondant roller
- pastry brush
- cake drum
- fondant smoother
- sharp knife
- edible glue
- edible or fabric ribbon

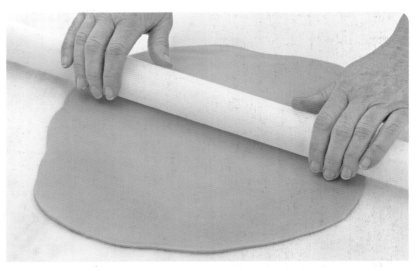

1 Dust a surface with cornflour and roll out the fondant into a circle 2mm (¹/₁₆in) thick and 30cm (12in) in diameter.

2 Use a pastry brush to apply a little water to the top and sides of the cake drum.

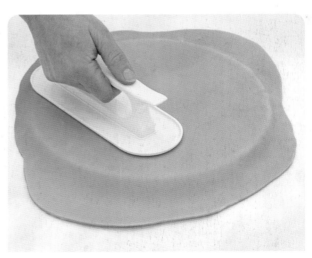

3 Lift the fondant onto the drum. Use a smoother to smooth from the centre outwards and around the sides. Trim off any excess fondant around the base. Allow to set overnight before placing your cake on top.

Icing

Vanilla buttercream icing

This traditional buttercream icing is softer and easier to spread than most icings. Its rich vanilla flavour and versatile consistency make it ideal for crumb coating, icing, and piping.

 PREP 15-20 mins   **MAKES** 750g (1lb 10oz)

Ingredients

- 250g (9oz) unsalted butter, softened
- 2 tsp vanilla extract
- 600g (1lb 5oz) icing sugar
- 2 tbsp double cream or milk, plus extra for thinning if needed
- colouring paste (optional)

Equipment

- electric whisk
- cocktail stick
- palette knife, for testing

1 Cream the butter and vanilla extract together with an electric whisk. Add the icing sugar, beating well. Finally, add in the cream or milk and continue mixing until the icing is light and fluffy.

2 Transfer the mix to a bowl. Dip a cocktail stick into the colouring paste, if using. Add just a dot of the colouring paste, a little at a time, until you achieve a uniform colour.

Colouring buttercream

Use colouring paste or gel rather than liquid colours to achieve a good consistency. The colours deepen over time, so use a tiny dab and blend before adding more.

3 The icing should be firm enough to hold a knife upright, but soft enough to be piped.

Chocolate buttercream

This icing works well with dark chocolate cakes. Follow step 1 of the vanilla buttercream recipe, using milk, not cream. Add 8 tablespoons of cocoa powder with the icing sugar and beat until fluffy. If you prefer a lighter flavour, halve the amount of cocoa powder and add a little more icing sugar.

Royal icing

This is the perfect recipe for royal icing that can be thinned slightly for detailed piping work, or used as glue for fondant decorations.

PREP 20 mins

MAKES 700g (1lb 9oz)

Ingredients
- 3 free-range pasteurized egg whites
- 1 tsp lemon juice, plus extra if needed
- 700g (1lb 9oz) icing sugar, sifted
- colouring paste (optional)

Equipment
- electric whisk
- cocktail stick

1 Whisk the egg whites in a large bowl and stir in the lemon juice. Gradually add the icing sugar and beat well.

2 Whisk until the icing has a smooth, toothpaste-like texture. Add more lemon juice if it is too thick.

3 Dip a cocktail stick into the colouring paste, if using. Add just a dot of colouring paste at a time, as a little goes a long way. Mix into the royal icing and stir until you achieve a uniform colour. The icing will last for up to 2 weeks, as long as it is kept well covered and refrigerated.

Piping

Fill your piping bag with royal icing, and keep the rest covered, with a damp towel, to prevent it from hardening. You may need to beat it again if it separates or a crust has formed.

Icing 181

Icing a cake

This method of icing can be used for buttercream, whipped cream, or ganache. Use side-scrapers to achieve a smooth or textured surface, or spread in swirls with a palette knife.

Ingredients
- cake, levelled, layered, and crumb coated (see pp170–171)
- buttercream icing (see p180)

Equipment
- cake board
- turntable or lazy Susan
- palette knife
- side scraper, flat-edged (optional)
- untextured kitchen paper

1 Carefully centre the crumb-coated cake on top of the cake board. Then, place it on a turntable and spoon a large amount of buttercream icing onto the centre of the cake.

2 With a palette knife, swirl and smooth the icing, spreading it outwards and over the sides as you go.

3 Turn the cake as you spread the icing down and around the sides of the cake, to cover it as evenly as possible. When it is smooth, allow the cake to set for about 10 minutes, and then repeat.

4 Fill a jug with boiling water and insert the palette knife into it. When it is hot, dry it and run it around the sides, turning the cake around, with the flat surface of the knife against the icing. Repeat until smooth.

5 Fill in any gaps with extra icing. Work on smoothing the top, turning the cake with the flat surface of the knife against the icing. Move from one side of the cake to the other, until it is smooth.

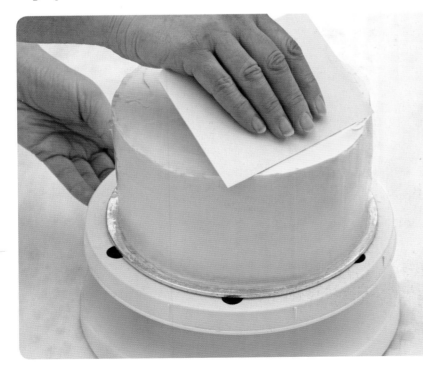

6 Alternatively, use the side scraper to smooth the icing first on the top, then dragging any excess icing down the sides. Smooth the sides in a single motion all the way around the cake.

setting

Always allow buttercream icing to set for at least 30 minutes before decorating, and even overnight, to create a really firm surface for your cake creations.

Tools and Equipment

You can use these widely available specialist tools and equipment to achieve different effects, textures, decorative touches, and perfect finishes for your birthday cakes. Start with the essentials and build your toolkit from there.

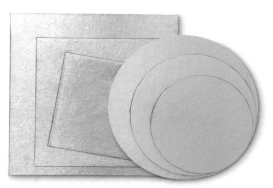

Cake boards and drums are available in different shapes and sizes. Thin cake boards support individual cakes for multiple tiers, and thicker drums provide a sturdy base.

Piping bags come in a variety of sizes. Choose larger ones to pipe buttercream icing on cakes or cupcakes, and smaller ones for more detailed work with royal icing.

Stitching (quilting) tools are used to emboss decorations and cakes with stitching effects.

Fondant rollers are essential for ensuring that fondant, flower paste, and other modelling clays are smooth and evenly rolled.

Metal cutters help cut accurate shapes that can be layered or used as the basis for decorations. Many come in sets of multiple sizes.

Plunger cutters create crisp shapes that are released with the touch of a button. Some also emboss the surface.

Round piping tips are versatile and widely used. They come in many sizes, from tiny tips for piping dots to wider tips for prominent effects.

Petal piping tips are available in many sizes, and help to create realistic flower petals, as well as ruffles, drapes, swags, and bows with royal or buttercream icing.

Open star piping tips are perfect for piped borders, single drops of stars and flowers, and swirled cupcakes.

Icing scrapers, with different edges, help to achieve a smooth or textured finish with buttercream or royal icing.

Paintbrushes come in many shapes and sizes. Use small brushes for fine details and larger ones for painting expanses of colour and dusting. Choose synthetic paintbrushes that will not lose their bristles.

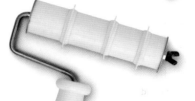

Dowels are cut to size and used to support heavy decorations or multiple cake tiers.

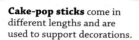

Cake-pop sticks come in different lengths and are used to support decorations.

Multi-ribbon cutters make cutting accurate lengths and strips of fondant or other pastes easy. Choose the width and fix the frame with interchangeable cutters that can emboss and/or cut decorative edges.

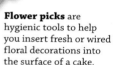

Flower picks are hygienic tools to help you insert fresh or wired floral decorations into the surface of a cake.

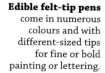

Fondant smoothers smooth decorations, boards, or cake toppings. Use two to achieve crisp corners and edges.

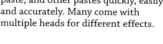

Ball tools can thin and soften edges to create natural petal shapes and contours.

Veining tools, also known as Dresden tools, add detail to fondant or paste decorations.

Wheel tools help cut fondant, flower paste, and other pastes quickly, easily, and accurately. Many come with multiple heads for different effects.

Edible felt-tip pens come in numerous colours and with different-sized tips for fine or bold painting or lettering.

Shell and blade tools help create shell patterns and textures for decorations.

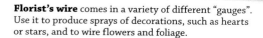

Florist's wire comes in a variety of different "gauges". Use it to produce sprays of decorations, such as hearts or stars, and to wire flowers and foliage.

Adapting Quantities

To adapt recipes for cakes of any size and shape, multiply the batches of batter you make. Check the packaging that came with novelty tins to ensure that you make the correct amount of batter and bake for the appropriate period of time.

	Cake tin	Multiple of vanilla sponge cake recipe	Fondant to cover	Bake time for sponge recipe at 180°C (160°C fan/350°F/Gas 4)
Round tins	13 x 6cm (5$\frac{1}{2}$ x 2$\frac{1}{2}$in)	1	400g (14oz)	15–20 mins
	15 x 6cm (6 x 2$\frac{1}{2}$in)	1	500g (1lb 2oz)	20–35 mins
	18 x 7cm (7 x 2$\frac{3}{4}$in)	1$\frac{1}{2}$	700g (1lb 8oz)	30–35 mins
	20 x 7.5cm (8 x 3in)	2	800g (1$\frac{3}{4}$lb)	35–40 mins
	23 x 8cm (9 x 3$\frac{1}{4}$in)	2$\frac{1}{2}$	900g (2lb)	40–45 mins
	25.5 x 9cm (10 x 3$\frac{1}{2}$in)	3$\frac{1}{2}$	1.1kg (2$\frac{1}{2}$lb)	50–55 mins
Square tins	15 x 6cm (6 x 2$\frac{1}{2}$in)	1$\frac{1}{2}$	700g (1lb 8oz)	30–35 mins
	18 x 7cm (7 x 2$\frac{3}{4}$in)	2	800g (1$\frac{3}{4}$lb)	35–40 mins
	20 x 7.5cm (8 x 3in)	2$\frac{1}{2}$	900g (2lb)	40–45 mins
	23 x 8cm (9 x 3$\frac{1}{4}$in)	3$\frac{1}{2}$	1.1kg (2$\frac{1}{2}$lb)	50–55 mins
	25.5 x 9cm (10 x 3$\frac{1}{2}$in)	5	1.25kg (2$\frac{3}{4}$lb)	1 hr–1 hr 5 mins
	28 x 9.5cm (11 x 3$\frac{3}{4}$in)	5	1.5kg (3lb 3oz)	1 hr 5 mins–1 hr 10 mins
	30 x 10cm (12 x 4in)	6	2kg (4$\frac{1}{2}$lb)	1 hr 10 mins
Bowl (hemisphere) tins	10cm (4in)	1	400g (14oz)	40–50 mins
	15cm (6in)	2	500g (1lb 2oz)	45–60 mins
	20cm (8in)	3$\frac{1}{2}$	750g (1lb 10oz)	1–1$\frac{1}{4}$ hrs

Templates

Use these simple templates to achieve accurate patterns for your birthday cakes and decorations. Enlarge the templates according to the percentage given here, using a photocopier or scanner, then print and cut them out, or trace and enlarge the templates by hand.

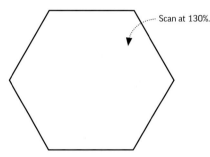

Scan at 130%.

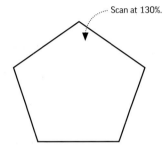

Scan at 130%.

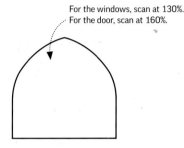

For the windows, scan at 130%.
For the door, scan at 160%.

Hexagon shape Scan, cut out, and use to cover the football in the Football Mania cake (p96).

Pentagon shape Scan, cut out, and use to cover the football in the Football Mania cake (p96).

Window shape Scan, cut out, and use to create windows and doors for the Princess Castle cake (p146).

For the skirt, scan at 130%.
For the bodice, scan at 120%.

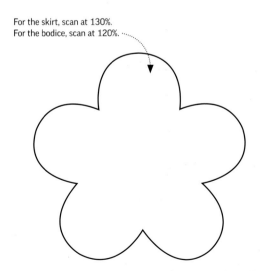

Scan at 170%.

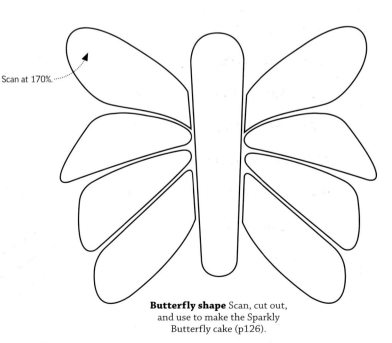

Flower shape Scan, cut out, and create floral skirts for the fairies in the Pretty Fairies cake (p20).

Butterfly shape Scan, cut out, and use to make the Sparkly Butterfly cake (p126).

Index

Acknowledgments

Author's acknowledgments

It has been a great pleasure to work with such a talented and inspiring group of people on this book. In particular, I'd like to thank our brilliant team of cake-makers: Sandra Monger, Kasey Clark, Hannah Wiltshire, Felicity Dodsworth and Krystle Drewry. Their gorgeous cakes, cupcakes, and cake pops speak for themselves. Sandra was responsible for supervising most of the step-by-step photography and was completely invaluable. Huge thanks also go to inspired editor Kathy Woolley and endlessly creative designer Harriet Yeomans. Thanks also to Peggy Vance, Dawn Henderson, Christine Keilty, and the DK team for faith and brilliance.

DK would like to thank Karen Sullivan, Sandra Monger, Hannah Wiltshire, Kasey Clarke, Felicity Dodsworth and Krystle Drewry for their cake contributions.
They would also like to thank:

Photography Ian O'Leary
Art Direction Susan Downing
Prop styling Isabel de Cordova
Hand model Jenny Volich
Proofreading Claire Cross
Indexing Vanessa Bird

About the contributors

Karen Sullivan is a custom cake-maker with a successful celebration cake business. She learned to bake as a toddler, in her grandmother's kitchen in Canada, and has honed her decorating skills over the years. She creates unique and highly sought-after cakes for a range of customers and occasions.

Sandra Monger is an award-winning cake designer who specializes in custom celebration cakes. Professionally trained in advanced pâtisserie and sugar craft, she also teaches cake-decorating courses.
www.sandramongercakes.co.uk

Hannah Wiltshire is a writer and cake expert with a particular interest in beautiful baking. She runs her cake business, Baby Cakes, from her home in Bath, England. She was a judge at the Cake and Bake Show in Earls Court, London.
www.bathbabycakes.com

Kasey Clarke created Kupkase in her family kitchen, and it has since grown into a nation-wide business. She's been a finalist at the National Cupcake Awards and has designed unique celebration cakes for a mix of high-profile clients and celebrities.
www.kupkase.com

Juniper Cakery is owned by Felicity Dodsworth and Krystle Drewry in Kingston upon Hull, England. Along with their head baker, Carol, they create custom celebration cakes and party confections, specializing in delicious cupcakes. They've designed and baked creations for Tala and The Happy Egg Co.
www.junipercakery.co.uk